This is a very timely and important study. Many
experts are asking a lot of questions about mari W9-BPM-516
a dearth of in-depth information and relevant policy proposals. This is a
crucial problem for Southeast Asia because the Malacca and Singapore straits
are very important waterways, through which one quarter of world trade
and half its oil go.

The scenarios outlined by Richardson on possible terrorist acts — a
nuclear explosive device or a 'dirty bomb' with a lot of radioactive fallout,
or making international straits and waters unsafe or impossible to use —
are indeed very dramatic possibilities. The use of ships or cargo containers
by terrorists is highly probable, and the world is not adequately prepared.
Government officials, experts, the private sector and scholars on terrorism
must read this significant essay. It is an eye-opener.

Jusuf Wanandi,
Chairman of the Supervisory Board,
Centre for Strategic and International Studies,
Jakarta, Indonesia.

Michael Richardson has done us all a great service by exposing a danger
that has needed more public attention. Al-Qaeda and other terrorist
networks can be counted on to know the weak links in the barriers that
have been set up to prevent nuclear proliferation. They probably knew that
the Pakistani scientist, A.Q. Khan, was selling the machinery, materials and
blueprints for atomic bomb-making.

But how to deliver such a bomb to a high-value target? It's not much
of a stretch to conclude that a fanatical terrorist network could use the
world's merchant marine to smuggle a primitive atom bomb into any one
of several major port cities around the world. If such a bomb were exploded,
the loss of life would be hundreds of times greater than those suffered by
the United States on 9/11. Even radioactive materials scattered by
conventional high explosives in a 'dirty bomb' would close down for a long
time that part of a city where the bomb was planted.

How can this avenue of attack be blocked without disrupting the vital
lifelines of maritime transportation? You can best consider this dilemma
while reading Richardson's balanced and comprehensive analysis.

James E. Goodby,
former chief nuclear arms negotiator for the United States government,
now affiliated with the Center for Northeast Asian Policy Studies at the
Brookings Institution

Michael Richardson's book is immensely important. It should be read by
policymakers and responsible people around the world, including Japan
where maritime security is of vital importance. Richardson, a veteran
Australian journalist long based in Singapore, does not just diagnose the
challenge laid down by Al-Qaeda, but makes timely recommendations about
what needs to be done — urgently.

Hideaki Kaneda,
retired Vice-Admiral of the Japan Maritime Self-Defence Force, and
Director of The Okazaki Institute for security policy studies in Tokyo.

Cover photograph:
This file picture dated 6 October 2002 shows a cloud of smoke billowing from French supertanker *Limburg* off the coast of the southeastern Yemeni port of al-Mukalla, 700 km east of Aden, after an explosion ripped through the supertanker killing one and injuring twelve others. Major seaports in Asia, North America and Europe are stepping up security amid fears that ships might become terrorists' next killer carriers of choice after airplanes, truck bombs, and now trains following the 11 March 2004 blasts in Madrid that killed nearly 200 people. Experts fear that terrorists could use ships to transport operatives, equipment or weapons, raise money through legal or illicit trade, and attack larger vessels like the *USS Cole*, also attacked in Yemen in 2000, or the *Limburg* attack, which is suspected of being caused by a link to the al-Qaeda terror network.

A Time Bomb for
Global Trade

The Institute of Southeast Asian Studies (ISEAS) was established as an autonomous organization in 1968. It is a regional centre dedicated to the study of socio-political, security and economic trends and developments in Southeast Asia and its wider geostrategic and economic environment.

The Institute's research programmes are the Regional Economic Studies (RES, including ASEAN and APEC), Regional Strategic and Political Studies (RSPS), and Regional Social and Cultural Studies (RSCS).

ISEAS Publications, an established academic press, has issued more than 1,000 books and journals. It is the largest scholarly publisher of research about Southeast Asia from within the region. ISEAS Publications works with many other academic and trade publishers and distributors to disseminate important research and analyses from and about Southeast Asia to the rest of the world.

A Time Bomb for Global Trade

Maritime-related Terrorism in an Age
of Weapons of Mass Destruction

Michael Richardson

INSTITUTE OF SOUTHEAST ASIAN STUDIES
Singapore

First published in Singapore in 2004 by
ISEAS Publications
Institute of Southeast Asian Studies
30 Heng Mui Keng Terrace, Pasir Panjang
Singapore 119614

E-mail: publish@iseas.edu.sg   • Website: bookshop.iseas.edu.sg

ISEAS Library Cataloguing-in-Publication Data

Richardson, Michael.
A time bomb for global trade : maritime-related terrorism in an age of
    weapons of mass destruction.
    1. Terrorism—Economic aspects.
    2. International trade—Effect of terrorism on.
    3. Shipping—Safety measures.
    I. Title.
    II. Title: Maritime-related terrorism in an age of weapons of mass
        destruction
HV6431 R52   2004

ISBN 981-230-246-8 (soft cover)

Typeset by International Typesetters Pte Ltd
Printed in Singapore by Seng Lee Press

Contents

Foreword

The threat of terrorism has escalated severalfold since terrorists struck the United States on 11 September 2001. Instead of an average of one attack by Al-Qaeda every year, post-9/11 Al-Qaeda and its associated groups stage an average of one attack every three months. Both before and after 9/11, Al-Qaeda successfully attacked or attempted to attack naval and commercial shipping of the US, its allies or its friends. After an aborted attempt to target *USS The Sullivans* in January 2000, Al-Qaeda nearly sank the state-of-the-art destroyer *USS Cole* in October 2000. Two years later, when a US warship failed to appear in a pre-designated kill zone of Al-Qaeda off Yemen, an explosives-laden boat piloted by an Al-Qaeda member struck a target of opportunity — the French oil supertanker *Limburg*.

As a learning organization, Al-Qaeda maximized its successes and minimized its failures. As the "pioneering vanguard of the Islamic movements", Al-Qaeda also instilled in its associated groups the important belief that they must repeat its successes. The international alert and publicity generated by these two iconic attacks led Al-Qaeda and its associated groups to invest extensively in developing technologies, tactics and techniques for conducting maritime terrorist operations. This was confirmed by the recovery in Afghanistan of video tapes for Asian, Middle Eastern, African and Caucasian terrorist groups to study in depth both offensive and defensive maritime operations by governments as well as by other terrorist groups. The clips of US warships in the Gulf, marine police patrolling the Malacca Strait, and maritime attacks by the Liberation Tigers of Tamil Eelam, the masters of maritime guerrilla and terrorist operations, were among the 241 videos recovered from the Al-Qaeda registry in Afghanistan.

Our knowledge of terrorist intentions, capabilities, and their opportunities for attack, increased after the US invasion of

Afghanistan in October 2001. Terrorist training manuals and attack plans specifically targeting naval and commercial maritime shipping in Asia, the Gulf and in the Mediterranean were recovered from the caves of Afghanistan and safe houses in Pakistan. Some of the training manuals both of Al-Qaeda and its associated groups, especially Harkat-ul-Mujahidin, demonstrated that the contemporary terrorist had developed extensive knowledge for conducting surface and underwater maritime attacks. Debriefings by American and Allied intelligence officers of several Al-Qaeda members and important leaders tasked to conduct maritime terrorist attacks revealed that the terrorists were only at a very early stage of exploiting the maritime domain.

The capture of Abdulrahim Mohammed Abda al Nishiri alias Mullah Ahmed Belal alias the Prince of the Sea, the Al-Qaeda head of Maritime Operations, and his supervisor Tawfiq bin Attash, the Deputy Head of Al-Qaeda operations, led to a greater understanding in the international intelligence community of the growing maritime threat. Worldwide, a dozen maritime attacks by Al-Qaeda and its associated groups from Turkey to the Straits of Gibraltar and from Indonesia to the Malacca Strait have been disrupted or aborted due to heightened security measures and countermeasures. These operations included plans to attack American and British warships in the Straits of Gibraltar using Morocco as a launching pad; strike cruise ships; sink a freighter in the Straits of Hormuz; kill American sailors in Malaysia; and to hit US naval vessels off Turkey, Singapore and Indonesia.

Although Al-Qaeda and its associated groups have suffered in the past two and a half years, the capacity of violent Islamist groups for adaptation and regeneration has ensured the continuity of the threat. Al-Qaeda has been transformed from a group into a movement of two dozen groups. Despite the death and capture of nearly 3,500 Al-Qaeda members out of an estimated 4,000 in October 2001, Al-Qaeda has become a force multiplier. In its place, two dozen violent Islamist groups have emerged as the principal threat. They received Al-Qaeda finance, training and ideology. Some of the associated groups are as capable as Al-Qaeda and prepared to use its techniques. For instance, the Singapore Chief of Jemaah Islamiyah was willing to hijack an Aeroflot plane from the International Airport in Bangkok and crash it into Changi International Airport in Singapore. In addition to Al-Qaeda, maritime-capable terrorist groups include Jemaah Islamiyah and the Abu Sayyaf Group in Southeast Asia, Islamic Army of the Abayan Aden, the Moroccan Islamic Combatant Group, and Salafi Group for Call and Combat in Algeria.

Most terrorist groups use the maritime environment not to conduct attacks but for support operations, to move men and material. It is not hard for any terrorist group to replicate land technologies in the maritime domain. So it is likely that groups which have traditionally been based on land will also mount terrorist attacks at sea when the need arises. Therefore, it is important for governments to watch maritime-capable groups engaged in support, as well as attack, operations. Increasingly, more such groups are developing underwater diving capabilities. A few, like the Moro Islamic Liberation Front and the Liberation Tigers of Tamil Eelam, have even attempted to acquire mini submarines. There is a growing sophistication of terrorist air, land and sea capabilities. Intelligence agencies and law enforcement authorities should develop specialized knowledge so that they can understand and operate more effectively in these domains.

Since 9/11, the international response to terrorism has not helped much to reduce the threat of terrorism. If the international community continues only to target the physical infrastructure of terrorist groups, it will fail to defeat terrorism. As government responses are kinetic, rather than ideological, the terrorist intention to kill in large numbers has not diminished. It is also important to target the conceptual infrastructure — the belief that it is the duty of every good Muslim to wage jihad.

Terrorists are being denied access to conventional weapons. As a result, they are increasingly looking to acquire commercially available technologies and unconventional weapon systems. For example, an Al-Qaeda associate group — the Tunisian Islamic Combatant Group — conducted an attack on the oldest Jewish Synagogue in Djerba, Tunisia, using a Liquid Petroleum Gas (LPG) vehicle. The attack killed 14 Germans, three Frenchmen, and five Tunisians. A convert to Islam, Jose Padilla, an American member of Al-Qaeda, is under arrest in the US for allegedly planning to use a radiological bomb in a major city. This kind of bomb, or even a crude nuclear explosive device, could be smuggled on board a ship and detonated inside a port.

If we are to better understand and respond to the threat of terrorism, we must think and act outside the box. Traditionally, the specialists on terrorism research believed that it was not within the capability of a non-state group to develop or acquire nuclear weapons. More recently, they have concluded that terrorists will manufacture and employ a radiological bomb that uses conventional explosives to disperse radioactive poison. Although nuclear weapon facilities were well guarded during the Cold War, this may not be the case today. The recruitment of scientists and technical specialists by terrorist groups as well as the terrorist-criminal nexus is likely to change the status quo. Coupled with the failure of most ports to profile ships and containers for terrorism risks and the growing terrorist intent to acquire and use nuclear and radiological weapons, the likelihood of an unconventional terrorist attack is increasing. With the enhanced security of the aviation and the land domains, the maritime domain is increasingly becoming vulnerable to terrorist penetration and attack.

This book on maritime terrorism is important for two reasons: First, there is no publicly available study on the contemporary wave of maritime terrorism. Throughout the Cold War, the threat of maritime terrorism was considered a low probability and a low impact form of attack. After 9/11, with terrorism moving from a public nuisance and a law and order problem to a national security threat, the risk rating for maritime terrorism has altered. Nonetheless, the investment to protect mobile and static maritime assets has been low and imprudent. Both the academic community and maritime security professionals have failed to examine the threat comprehensively. Richardson's study is an important first step in helping both the public and the private sectors to start thinking seriously about the problem.

Second, as the sea is the least policed domain, maritime assets are vulnerable to terrorist attack. This book provides an accurate description of the extant and emerging threat. Before onshore and offshore targets are struck by a wave of maritime attacks, the international community must develop a range of mechanisms to prevent, protect and respond to the threat. As the threat of maritime terrorism is complex and will not diminish in the short term, there is no singular approach to dealing with the threat. With the help of the shipping community, governments can reduce the threat of a maritime attack to manageable proportions by developing a multi-pronged, multi-agency, multi-jurisdictional and multi-national response.

ISEAS must be complimented for inviting Michael Richardson to write *A Time Bomb for Global Trade: Maritime-related Terrorism in an Age of Weapons of Mass Destruction*. The book is a must read for both the specialist and the general reader.

Rohan Gunaratna

Rohan Gunaratna is Head, International Centre for Political Violence and Terrorism Research at the Institute of Defence and Strategic Studies, Singapore. As a Senior Advisor to the Maritime Intelligence Group in Washington DC, he assisted in the development of the Vigilence Vessel Profiling System (VVPS).

Message from the Director

This timely book by Michael Richardson provides a useful overview of the current issues and trends in the field of maritime security; he also provides some practical recommendations to strengthen overall security and to rectify some grave weaknesses in the system. Both practitioners and the public will find his book an interesting and timely warning of the potential dangers of mass-casualty maritime terrorism. Richardson clearly highlights some linkages between piracy and maritime terrorism. With land-based targets harder to get at, the attention of terrorist groups could turn to the maritime sector.

Mega-hub ports and major container terminals, such as Singapore, are vulnerable to trade disruptions and blockages of access to sealanes. Such disruptions caused by maritime terrorism will be very damaging to their economies and to the global economy. The example of the impact of maritime terrorism on the Port of Aden, in the aftermath of the terrorist attack on the French tanker *Limburg*, demonstrates that even a failed attack can devastate a port economy. Fully alerted to the dangers, Singapore and some other ports in the region have adopted strong security measures to increase port security. These include the rule that large cargo vessels and passenger ships must be fitted with automatic identification systems that can transmit data to port authorities. Singapore has gone further in requiring all vessels, including small harbour crafts, to be fitted with such transponders. Thus, Singapore will be one of the first countries to be classified by the IMO as a secure port, which means that ships sailing from here will have no problems going to another port.

Much of the world's oil exports and trade pass through the Straits of Malacca and Singapore. The littoral states, and the international community at large, are acutely aware of the dangers of both these waterways becoming choke-points to maritime trade in the event of terrorist actions undertaken at sea.

Against this background, ISEAS has developed a programme on issues relating to maritime security. Richardson's book is the precursor to further research into an increasingly vital area of concern to the international community.

K. Kesavapany
Director,
ISEAS.

Preface

This book aims to answer these questions:

- Are Al-Qaeda, the world's most feared terrorist network, and like-minded extremist groups interested in using ships, ports, and the sea and land links in the global cargo container supply chain, for their own purposes?
- Is one of their aims to use a ship or container as a weapon to attack a major port-city or disrupt traffic in a key strait or waterway for international shipping, possibly using a nuclear or radiological bomb?
- If so, could such an attack slow or even halt seaborne trade, a vital engine of the world economy?
- What is being done to counter threats of maritime terrorism and how effective are the safeguards?

These questions may sound melodramatic. But the evidence gathered in this book shows that the threats to seaborne trade and its land connections, including ports and adjacent cities, are very serious and are being treated as such by knowlegeable officials, private sector executives and security analysts in North America, Asia, Europe and Australasia whose countries, trade, assets and people abroad may become terrorist targets.

Much is now known about the operations and plans on land and in the air of Al-Qaeda, its affiliates and emulators. This has been widely publicized. But less is known about the maritime-related activities of terrorist organizations which this book documents. Governments around the world are concerned not only that Al-Qaeda and like-minded terrorist groups will strike more frequently, but that they may strike with more powerful weapons in new ways, including via the sea.

As this book makes clear, Al-Qaeda aims to disrupt the seaborne trading system, the backbone of the modern global economy, and would use a crude nuclear explosive device or a radiological bomb to do so if it could get its hands on either and position it to go off in a port-city, shipping strait or waterway that plays a key role in international trade.

This book does not cover chemical or biological weapons, although both are of interest to Al-Qaeda and other extremist groups. While terrorists might use ships or cargo containers to smuggle chemical or biological weapons or poisons into a country for an attack, these toxins could not be effectively dispersed by ship or container and would need to be offloaded for final use. By contrast, terrorists with nuclear or radiological bombs that were brought to their target by sea would use the ship or container to hide, deliver and detonate the device.

The book does not deal with the risk of terrorists attacking cruise liners or offshore oil or gas fields and installations. Both are a real possibility and could cause many hundreds of casualties and much localized damage. The risk for cruise liners has been obvious since the *Achille Lauro* was hijacked by Palestinian terrorists in 1985, but neither of these maritime terrorism possibilities has the potential to disrupt world trade unless a cruise liner was sunk, scuttled or exploded in the way this book defines for other ships involved in a mega-terror plot.

1 Trade, Terrorists, Shipping, and Cargo Containers

Are sea container shipping and its land links in the global supply chain vulnerable to a major terrorist attack? Many officials in the United States, Asia and Europe believe so. Here are some samples:

> The system is vulnerable to exploitation by international terrorist organisations. A cargo container loaded up with any kind of nuclear or radiological weapon would have a potentially catastrophic effect, not only in loss of life but to the US economy and the economies of every trading nation in the world. While the threat is hopefully small, the effects could be so great that anybody in my position would have to be concerned.[1]

> Robert Bonner, US Customs and Border Protection Commissioner

> One major challenge to the marine industry is global terrorism. The 9/11 attacks, and subsequently the discovery of the Jemaah Islamiyah group in Singapore, showed that terrorism is a problem of global scale. Terrorists are operating through international networks. There is growing concern that their next attack may be via ships and shipping containers. This would not only inflict heavy casualties and damage to property, but also disrupt the wheels of international commerce. This can potentially cripple international trade...

> Lee Hsien Loong, Deputy Prime Minister of Singapore[2]

> The massive flow of containers around the world makes global maritime transport an essential part of the world economy and makes it almost impossible to picture the disastrous consequences which a terrorist attack would have on global freight supply systems. Borders would be closed; ships might not be allowed to enter ports.

There would be a complete disruption of the global supply chain with enormous consequences for the global economy.[3]

Frits Bolkestein, European Commission member in charge of the EU's Internal Market, Taxation and Customs.

What's at Stake and Why?

Given the vast scale of the global shipping and cargo container industry and its vulnerability to acts of terrorism, better security is vital when the risk of weapons of mass destruction reaching international terrorists is rising.

Improving maritime security is especially important for the United States and Canada, member states of the European Union, Australia and New Zealand, and for China, Japan, South Korea, Taiwan, Thailand, Malaysia and other economies in East Asia that have extensive direct seaborne trade with other industrialized nations. It is doubly vital for places like Singapore, Hong Kong and Rotterdam that are not only very large seaports with global connections, but also giant container trans-shipment hubs.

Asia-Pacific Stake

China and many other Asia-Pacific economies that have industrialized rapidly in the past few decades depend heavily on seaborne trade. Asia controls and operates more than 40 per cent of the global commercial fleet, supplies the vast majority of its crews, and builds most of its ships. Many of the world's biggest ports are in East Asia and much of the traffic they handle passes through the key straits of Southeast Asia.

Over a quarter of the world's trade and half its oil go through the Straits of Malacca and Singapore. The energy and raw materials that traverse Southeast Asian straits keep the economies of Japan, greater China and South Korea humming. China has become the dynamo for Japan, South Korea, Australia and many Southeast Asian economies, providing them with a rapidly expanding market even as it competes for foreign investment and in exports. China became the world's fourth largest merchandise trader in 2002, after the US, Japan and the EU. It has recently overtaken Japan to become the second biggest oil importer, after the US. Without reliable seaborne trade, including oil supplies, the Northeast Asian regional economy would slow drastically, if not grind to a halt. Much of Australia's trade is with East Asia and goes by sea through Southeast Asian straits. The Asia-Pacific stake in maritime security is therefore huge.[4]

The Twin Achilles Heels of Global Trade

Seaborne trade is vulnerable to a well planned terrorist attack on two fronts:

- the port-city hubs that form an interdependent global trading web and increasingly dominate container shipping;
- the handful of international straits and canals through which 75 per cent of world maritime trade passes. These waterways are relatively narrow and could be blocked, at least temporarily.

Shipping is the heart of global trade. World merchandise exports were worth US$6,270 billion in 2002. Most international trade — about 80 per cent of the total by volume — is carried by sea. World maritime trade set a record in 2002, reaching almost 5.9 billion metric tons, including oil and bulk commodities, and general cargo packed mainly in containers. About half the world's trade by value, and 90 per cent of the general cargo, is transported in containers — standardized steel boxes that are usually 20-feet or 40-feet long, and are commonly referred to as "twenty-foot equivalent units" (TEUs) or "forty-foot equivalent units" (FEUs).

Port-City Hubbing

An ever greater proportion of container shipping trade is being concentrated in giant ports with the modern facilities to handle the boxes. The top 20 container terminals in 2002, led by Hong Kong, Singapore and four other East Asian ports, accounted for 54 per cent of world sea container throughput in 2002 — 127 million TEUs out of a total of 237 million TEUs. In 2000, the top 20 terminals handled 109 million TEUs, 47 per cent of the global total of 232 million TEUs. As the ships that carry containers on long voyages become larger to take advantage of economies of scale, many of the leading terminals act as transhipment points for smaller ships and regional ports in a hub-and-spoke system.[5]

Chokepoints

The smooth operation of the global economy also depends on the free flow of shipping through international straits, waterways and canals. Seventy-five per cent of global maritime trade passes through a handful of relatively narrow shipping lanes. Nearly 35 million barrels of oil per day — just under half the world's daily consumption of nearly 78 million barrels in 2002 — passes through six geographic "chokepoints", or narrow channels. A growing proportion of the global trade in liquified natural gas (LNG), another key energy source for Japan, South Korea and increasingly for other countries, is carried through some of the same channels:

- Strait of Hormuz leading out of the Persian Gulf to the Arabian Sea and Indian Ocean;
- Malacca and Singapore Straits linking the Indian Ocean (and oil and gas supplies from the Middle East) with the Pacific Ocean (and major consuming markets in Asia) via the Andaman Sea and the South China Sea;
- Panama Canal connecting the Pacific and Atlantic Oceans;
- Suez Canal linking the Red Sea and the Mediterranean Sea;
- Bab el-Mandab passage from the Arabian Sea and the Gulf of Aden to the Red Sea; and
- Bosporus and Turkish Straits, connecting the Black Sea and the Mediterranean.

These channels are critically important to the world's trade because so much of it passes through them. Yet they are also "chokepoints" because they are narrow enough to be closed for some time to commercial shipping, by an accident or by an attack, including a terrorist operation.[6]

Post-9/11 and the War on Terrorism

On 11 September 2001, Al-Qaeda used four hijacked jet airliners to kill nearly 3,000 people from 80 nations. Two of the planes were flown into the World Trade Center twin towers in New York, bringing both skyscrapers down. Another of the hijacked airliners crashed into the headquarters of the US Defense Department in Washington. They were stunning strikes on the centres of financial and political power in the US.[7]

The use of civilian planes as weapons to strike New York and Washington fundamentally changed approaches to transport security. It exposed a whole new degree of vulnerability in the global transport system. Following the attacks, the US shut its air space for four days and its ports for two days. Border crossings were closed along the frontier with Canada, where half a million vehicles cross daily, leading to severe delays. Some companies dependent on just-in-time deliveries experienced a breakdown in their supply chains. New security measures were introduced, initially for aviation but later for other forms of transport as well, including shipping, ports and cargo containers.[8]

The Bush administration has poured billions of dollars into tighter airline security, mainly to improve checks of passengers and their baggage. Some US officials fear that the next big attack on America could come by sea, not by air. Many officials in Asia, Australia, New Zealand and Europe share this concern about maritime-related terrorism. Al-Qaeda has said a number of times that it wants to shut key sealanes to strike a mortal blow at the political economy of the West.

From Land and Air to Sea

So far, terrorists have mainly used trucks and other motor vehicles packed with explosives, or fuel-laden aircraft, as their most destructive weapons. Now, one of the biggest concerns of authorities is that terrorists may strike using another vital form of transportation — ships and cargo containers.

Officials and counter-terrorism experts have warned that the next step up in mega-terrorism may be an attack using CBRN (chemical, biological, radiological or nuclear weapons). Some say that a radiological, or "dirty" bomb attack, using conventional explosives to disperse deadly radioactive material, is inevitable sooner or later.

Those who worry about such an attack believe that weapons of mass destruction and terrorism have become interlocking threats — and could, if effective safeguards are not put in place quickly, fuse in an extremely dangerous challenge to global security and stability. The exposure in February 2004 of an extensive and long-running nuclear black market that funnelled weapons technology to Iran, Libya and North Korea from Pakistan has heightened these fears.[9]

The Labyrinth World: Shipping and Containers

Global shipping is an industry of vast scale and labyrinthine complexity. But the industry is not only vast; it is lightly regulated, frequently beyond the reach of the law and often secretive in its operations, especially in concealing the real owners of ships. Oceans cover 70 per cent of the world's surface and most of this huge area is classifed by law as international waters, or high seas, where ships are free to roam unhindered except in certain very specific circumstances. Despite a raft of new anti-terrorist measures that took effect in 2002 and 2003 and more that will be applied in 2004, the sea and the shipping industry remain an attractive domain for terrorist operations.[10]

Most seaborne international trade is carried by at least 46,000 ships calling at over 2,800 ports. There are more than 1.2 million seafarers and hundreds of thousands of port workers. Apart from ships and ports, the millions of uniform steel containers that carry most of today's general cargo around the world are a security nightmare. Once loaded and sealed, inspection is a problem. The contents of a container can be misrepresented and undeclared items hidden inside with relative ease. Even when sealed, containers can be surreptitiously opened and then closed again without great difficulty to remove or add contents. This is a made-to-order method of transport for terrorists — just as it is for drug and other contraband smugglers.

As many as 15 million containers are in circulation, criss-crossing the globe by sea and making over 230 million journeys through the world's ports each year. Some seven million containers arrive by sea in US ports alone each year. They carry goods worth more than US$730 billion. Checks of containers reaching American ports by sea increased to 5.2 per cent of total arrivals by September 2003, from 2 per cent two years earlier. But worldwide, less than 1 per cent of shipped cargo is screened using X-ray and gamma ray devices to peer inside for explosives, radioactive substances or other dangerous materials.[11]

2003

Sea–Land Links in the Global Supply Chain

Like the seaborne trading system, the global supply chain is vast, complex and vulnerable to terrorist infiltration and attack. There are some 40,000 freight forwarders worldwide who employ as many as 10 million people.

While most of the world's trade travels by sea, the ocean voyage is only one link in an extensive chain. A typical door-to-door journey for general cargo in a shipping container will involve some 25 different handlers, generate up to 40 different sets of documents, use several other transport modes like truck or rail, and pass through as many as 15 different locations, from the factory or warehouse where the goods are loaded into a container, to the point of unloading and delivery.[12]

Secure Trade vs Free Trade

The very nature and scale of the globalized trading system makes it vulnerable to terrorist attack. Seaborne trade and its land connections in the global supply chain have become increasingly open. They are liable to be targeted or exploited by terrorist groups that have the capability to strike in different parts of the world and aim to cause as much fear and chaos as possible to advance their ends.

In recent decades, the Asia-Pacific region has followed its main trade partners in North America and Europe in deregulating and encouraging freer trade and commerce, to foster economic growth. In the wake of the terrorist attacks on the US in September 2001, and the subsequent plots and bombings in Indonesia and other parts of Southeast Asia, the region and its leading trade partners must tighten security at sea, in ports and throughout the logistic supply chains that have become critical to modern manufacturing and service industries.

The global economy is built on integrated supply chains that feed components and other materials to users just before they are required and just in the right amounts. That way, inventory costs are kept low. If the supply chains are disrupted, it will have repercussions around the world, profoundly affecting business confidence.

On the other hand, if security measures start to slow global trade significantly or make it much more expensive, the world economy will suffer. Striking the right balance between free trade and security is critically important, and it must be done in 2004 as a wide range of new counter-terrorist measures take effect.[13]

Benefits of Secure Trade

However, the new security measures, when effectively applied and extended on a more universal basis, could help streamline global commerce as well as giving it greater protection. The benefits, which can amount to significant savings, should include faster processing when containers reach US ports, lower insurance costs and fewer losses due to theft. The security requirements will make it more difficult to falsify identification of goods for customs declaration purposes. This will reduce the scope for corruption and cut transaction costs.

For example, estimated losses from cargo theft worldwide range from 30 billion US dollars per year to as high as 50 billion dollars. Most of the thefts involve cargo containers being transported by trucks. However, seaports and container staging areas are also prone to container cargo theft. The installation of container scanners in the Port of Rotterdam cost 15 million euros. But in one year, their use generated 88 million euros in customs and tax revenue that would otherwise have been lost, even though only 2 per cent of containers, on average, are subjected to checks in the port.[14]

Technology Innovation

One of the greatest potential benefits of the US-led drive to make container shipments more secure is the technology innovation it is spurring as governments and the private sector, increasingly in collaboration, seek new ways to overcome problems raised by fears of terrorism. A global seaborne transport system and supply chain network that are made more secure by advanced technology would be an enormous boon to trade, business and job creation.

Multinational companies and other trade-reliant firms have a vested interest in hastening this result because they do not want any interruption in the supply chain that would keep their goods out of world markets and cost them money. Even those who worry about the costs of meeting the new security requirements acknowledge that the potential damage from a major terrorist attack using ships or cargo containers could be many times higher than the costs of enhanced security.

Trojan Boxes

The world has not experienced a major terrorist attack using ships or containers — at least not yet. But it is clear that terrorists can see the potential of using the maritime trading system to conceal weapons or agents for attack purposes or to provide funding or support for their operations. Terrorists have used small, high-speed craft, packed with conventional explosives several times in recent years to cause serious damage to, and deaths on, much larger vessels.

Vessels, big and small, or the cargo containers they carry can be used in a number of ways by terrorists to further their aims:

- to raise money, through legal or illegal trade, to finance their activities;
- to covertly transport operatives, equipment and weapons to support terrorist operations;
- to deliver bombs or other means of destruction to their destination, such as in a container set to explode near a port-city or other target;
- to use vessels as weapons in their own right. Oil and chemical tankers could be sunk or set ablaze in a busy strait, waterway or port to cause pollution and disrupt shipping. Ammonium nitrate carriers or petroleum tankers could be rigged as floating bombs. Ammonium nitrate is a common agricultural fertilizer. It is widely traded around the world by sea. But it can, when mixed with fuel oil, be turned into

a powerful explosive. Packed into trucks, vans and cars, it has been used in many terrorist bombings.

Terrorists and Sea Transport

Al-Qaeda understands the vital role of sea transport and has exploited it for many years. The terrorist network has used cargo containers or ships to ferry agents and probably terrorist-related material around the world. Documents in Arabic, seized from one of Osama bin Laden's senior aides six years ago, show how Al-Qaeda intended to use containers packed with sesame seeds to smuggle highly radioactive material to the US.[15]

In August 2003, reports emerged that Al-Qaeda's director of global operations, Khalid Shaikh Mohammed, had offered to buy into a business that shipped garments in containers from Karachi to New York, shortly before he was captured in Pakistan in March 2003 in a raid directed by the US Central Intelligence Agency (CIA). At the time, US officials said that Mohammed, the alleged mastermind of the attacks on New York and Washington in September 2001, was planning new attacks on America but would not elaborate.[16]

Investing in the Future

Days before he was arrested, Khalid Shaikh Mohammed met in Karachi with Uzair Paracha, the son of the owner of a company in New York that imports clothing. Al-Qaeda's third highest-ranking figure, after Osama bin Laden and his deputy Ayman al-Zawahri, reportedly offered to invest about 200,000 US dollars in the firm, International Merchandise Group (IMG), in exchange for access to IMG's shipping containers bound for Port Newark in the New York-New Jersey harbour complex. IMG is an export-import company that ships clothing in containers to the US for clients, including Kmart.[17]

Details of the alleged plot came from the case brought by the US government against Uzair Paracha, the 23 year-old son of IMG's co-owner, Saifullah Paracha. Paracha Jr. has been detained by the US Federal Bureau of Investigation (FBI), since being picked up on 31st March 2003 at the IMG office in New York, shortly after he arrived from Pakistan. He was charged in a criminal complaint filed on 8 August 2003 with acting as cover for one of Khalid Shaikh Mohammed's associates — an Al-Qaeda operative identified in press reports as Majid Khan, although neither he nor Mohammed was identified in the indictment.[18]

US Attorney General John Ashcroft said that the case involving Uzair Paracha "demonstrates that Al-Qaeda will go to great lengths to enlist support here in the United States. Our efforts are focused on identifying and dismantling those rings of support on which our terrorist enemies seek to rely."[19]

Court papers filed by the FBI in the case against Paracha say that he met with two unnamed Al-Qaeda operatives in Karachi at least twice in February 2003 and that Paracha was told they "wanted to invest approximately US$200,000" in IMG.[20] From the time of the arrests, US Federal authorities monitored containers carrying IMG cargo to New York harbour but no weapons or destructive devices are known to have been found.

The US government filed a five-count indictment of Paracha on 8 October 2003 in which he was accused of "accepting up to US$200,000 of Al-Qaeda funds to be held as an investment in a business by which Paracha was employed, until such time as the funds were needed by Al-Qaeda".[21]

The indictment filed by US Attorney James Comey expanded the charges from one in the intial complaint to five: conspiracy to provide material support or resources to a foreign terrorist organization; providing and attempting to provide material support to a foreign terrorist organization; conspiracy to make or receive a contribution of funds, goods, or services, to and for the benefit of Al-Qaeda; making or receiving a contribution of funds, goods, or services to, and for the benefit of, Al-Qaeda; and identification document fraud.[22]

Behind the Scene

Although neither Khalid Shaikh Mohammed nor Majid Khan were named as the two Al-Qaeda operatives in the US government's criminal complaint against Uzair Paracha on 8 August, 2003, Paracha's lawyer Anthony Ricco was quoted as saying that information from Khalid Shaikh Mohammed to his US interrogators was behind the indictment. What he revealed led indirectly to Paracha's arrest.[23]

The other Al-Qaeda operative implicated in the conspiracy, Majid Khan, is a former Baltimore resident who allegedly conducted surveillance for the terrorist group in the US. Among other things, Paracha is said to have helped Khan obtain travel documents and posed as Khan when telephoning the US Immigration and Naturalization Service. FBI agents said that in Paracha's residence they found Khan's Maryland driver's licence, his

Social Security card, his Bank of America ATM card, and a key to his post office box.

Lawyers for Paracha, who has pleaded not guilty, said that his defence will hinge on their ability to have Khalid Shaikh Mohammed, the top Al-Qaeda captive in US custody, brought to court for questioning. They also want to question Majid Khan and Paracha's father. Judge Sidney Stein gave the defence six weeks from Paracha's arraignment in court on 14 October 2003 to present their motion. Paracha's father has been detained at the US airbase in Baghram, Afghanistan, since July. The places of detention of Khan and Khalid Shaikh Mohammed have not been publicly disclosed by US authorities.

Paracha's lawyers predict that his case is headed for the same legal standoff that caused an indefinite delay in the trial of Zacarias Moussaoui, the only US prosecution so far that is directly related to the terrorist attacks in the US in September 2001. Federal prosecutors are likely to oppose access to Khalid Shaikh Mohammed, as they have in the Moussaoui case, on national security grounds. Paracha's lawyers argue that without such access, Paracha's constitutional right to call available witnesses of his own choosing will be breached and he will not get a fair trial.[24]

Al-Qaeda's Stowaway

The fear that terrorists could exploit the container transport system was confirmed barely a month after the Al-Qaeda hijackers crashed civilian airliners into the World Trade Center twin towers and the Pentagon.

In October 2001, authorities in the southern Italian port of Gioia Tauro discovered an unusually well-equipped and neatly dressed stowaway locked inside a shipping container. It was furnished as a makeshift home with a bed, water, supplies for a long journey and a bucket for a toilet. Italian police named the stowaway as Rizik Amid Farid, 43, and said he was born in Egypt but carried a Canadian passport.

Unlike most stowaways, Farid was smartly dressed, clean-shaven and rested as he emerged. He was found to be carrying two mobile phones, a satellite phone, a laptop computer, several cameras, batteries and, ominously given recent events in the US, airport security passes and an airline mechanic's certificate valid for four major American airports. He had a return airline ticket from Montreal, Canada, to Egypt via Rome. Italian investigators said that the air ticket could be an "insurance policy" enabling him to reach

Canada by air in case he was discovered in the container but managed to escape.[25]

Gioia Tauro is a leading trans-shipment hub for cargo in the Mediterranean. The container fitted out as a makeshift home had been loaded in Port Said, Egypt. Had the stowaway not been trying to widen ventilation holes when workers in Gioia Tauro were nearby, the box may well have passed unhindered to its final destination in Canada via Rotterdam. After he was discovered, Farid was investigated by Italian prosecutors who suspected that he was an Al-Qaeda operative. He was charged with illegal entry into Italy and detained. But a court released him on bail and he disappeared before further information about him and the purpose of his unorthodox means of travel could be gathered.[26]

Since then, the suspected use of cargo containers by stowaway-terrorists has been a matter of official concern in the US and Europe. Senator Bob Graham, chairman of the US Senate Intelligence Committee has said that he knew of 25 "extremists" who sneaked onto ships bound for the US, hid in the cargo containers during the voyage, and then left the vessels when they docked and disappeared into population.[27]

2 Al-Qaeda's "Navy"

A terrorist alert in October 2003 triggered yet another search in the worldwide hunt for one of the ships and some of the crew that have been widely reported to be part of Al-Qaeda's undercover shipping line. Following an intelligence tip-off — said to be from the US — that some of the crew were linked to Al-Qaeda, New Zealand authorities raided a Greek-owned cargo ship, the *Athena*, in Lyttelton, the port of Christchurch in New Zealand. The freighter regularly carries logs, fertilizer and cement between New Zealand and Asia. It had arrived in Lyttelton on 2 October and was due to leave for South Korea two days later when customs officials gave it an unusually thorough inspection, including checks on the identities of all crew and a full search of the vessel. Nothing of concern was found, according to a customs spokeswoman.[1]

When the 17,000-ton *Athena* and its cargo of logs reached the port of Kunsan on the southwest coast of South Korea on 30 October, it was checked again by Korean authorities. They searched for weapons and forged passports but found nothing unusual on board. Some 37,000 US troops are based in South Korea and there are many American military facilities in Kunsan, including an airbase.[2]

Many Searches

There have been many such searches for Al-Qaeda-connected ships and crew since the terrorist attacks on the US in September 2001 made the US and many other countries aware of just how vulnerable the largely unregulated and secretive global maritime industry is to abuse by terrorists. These concerns were underscored on 21 December 2001, just a few weeks after the attacks on New York and Washington, when British anti-terrorist officers and naval commandos intercepted and boarded the *Nisha*, an Indian-owned bulk carrier, in the English

Channel. The vessel was carrying raw sugar to a refinery on the Thames, near London's Canary Wharf financial and residential district. British authorities said they were acting on an intelligence tip-off that the ship was carrying "terrorist material". But three days of searching found nothing suspicious and the *Nisha* was allowed to dock and unload at the Thames terminal in early January.[3]

A year later it was reported that US intelligence officials had identified approximately <u>15 cargo ships around the world that they</u> <u>believed were controlled by Al-Qaeda or could be used by the</u> <u>terrorist network to ferry operatives, bombs, money or commodities</u> over the high seas. American spy agencies were said to be monitoring some of the suspicious ships by satellites, surveillance planes, and with the help of allied navies or informants among overseas port managers, shipping agents, crew manning supervisors and seafarers unions. But US authorities sometimes lost track of the vessels, which were continually given new fictitious names, repainted or re-registered using invented corporate owners.

Tracking suspected terrorist vessels is difficult. Intelligence agents have to watch the world's 120,000 merchant ships in national as well as international trade, many of which hide their ownership under layers of corporate subterfuge. Intelligence officers also must collate the names and mariner's licence numbers of tens of thousands of seamen from around the world, a sizable percentage of whom carry fake documents and use false names.[4]

Bombs and Drugs

US officials and security analysts fear that Al-Qaeda could use any ships it owns, leases or controls not just to make money from carrying commercial cargo, but for group logistics or in terrorist operations to ferry bombs, operatives, money and materials.[5]

The first reports of Al-Qaeda-linked ships emerged in late 2001. Several shipping companies were thought to be owned or managed by people with ties to the Al-Qaeda network. America's CIA and the Norwegian security service, with the help of international shipping registries, had combined to try to identify the suspect ships. While some were large ocean-going vessels, others were small nondescript freighters, dhows (Arab sailing boats), and yachts that were used to carry supplies, weapons and people around the waters of Southwest Asia, North Africa and the Middle East.[6]

One Al-Qaeda vessel delivered the explosives that its operatives used to bomb two US embassies in East Africa in August 1998, killing 224 people, nearly all Africans (12 Americans were among the dead). US investigators say they have evidence that Al-Qaeda was buying ships at least as early as 1994. Wahid El-Hage, who was sentenced to life imprisonment on terrorism conspiracy charges in 2001 for his role in the bombing of the US embassies in Nairobi, Kenya, and Dar es Salaam, Tanzania, had bought a tramp freighter, the *Jennifer*, in April 1994. After the 1998 embassy bombings, the ship appears to have continued carrying legitimate cargoes around the Red Sea before it reportedly sank off the coast of Oman in 2000. The wreck of the ship, by then renamed *Sky 1*, was never found.[7]

In December 2003, US and allied forces on patrol in the Persian Gulf tracked and boarded several dhows, confiscating three drug shipments worth more than US$15 million. US officials said that 7 of the 45 crewmen detained had links to Al-Qaeda and that the organization was using drug smuggling to help finance its operations. The first shipment included nearly two metric tons of hashish; the second, 67 kilograms of methamphetamine, a stimulant drug; the third, 38 kilograms of heroin, although a much larger amount was believed to have been dumped overboard when the crew realized they were about to be searched.

Government officials and terrorism analysts have long believed that Al-Qaeda was getting funds through criminal enterprises, including the drug trade. Before the attacks on the US in September 2001, Al-Qaeda leader Osama bin Laden had been sheltered in Afghanistan by the Taliban, which was linked to the international trade in heroin derived from Afghanistan's opium poppy crops.

Ironically, since the US-led invasion of Afghanistan to get rid of Al-Qaeda and their Taliban allies, production of hashish, opium and the heroin refined from it, have risen sharply again, apparently under the protection of some regional warlords and their private armies whose support the US needs. About 3,400 metric tons of opium was produced in Afghanistan in 2002. The 2003 harvest was expected to be even greater: some 4,000 metric tons, accounting for approximately 75 per cent of the world's supply. Iran and the Persian Gulf are major transit routes for drugs from Afghanistan to markets in Europe and the oil-rich Gulf states.

Smaller terrorist groups linked to Al-Qaeda, such as Ansar al-Islam in Iraq and the Abu Sayyaf Group in the Philippines, also have been accused of involvement in the drug trade.

The seizures from the three dhows in the Persian Gulf in December 2003 were described in some reports as the first hard evidence of Al-Qaeda's involvement in illicit drug smuggling.

However, the US government had charged two Pakistan nationals and a US citizens in November 2002 with conspiring to exchange 600 kilograms of heroin and five metric tons of hashish for cash and four Stinger shoulder-fired anti-aircraft missiles. The US alleged that the defendants, who were arrested in Hong Kong, had admitted they intended to sell the missiles to Al-Qaeda forces in Afghanistan.[8]

Global Maritime Surveillance

Since September 2001, the US-maintained list of suspected Al-Qaeda ships has varied from a low of a dozen to a high of fifty. Meanwhile, America and its allies have mounted one of the largest naval seahunts and shipping surveillance operations since World War II to track and, if necessary, inspect "ships of concern".

Shortly after the terrorist attacks on the United States, the North Atlantic Treaty Organization (NATO) began naval and air patrols in the Mediterranean Sea to prevent possible terrorist activity on Europe's southern sea flank in an exercise known as Operation Active Endeavour. Airborne Warning and Control Systems (AWACs) aircraft are involved. Some 36,000 merchant vessels had been monitored by the end of October 2003. From April that year, some of the vessels were boarded to check that their cargo matched the items declared in their shipping manifests. In March, 2003, NATO warships began escorting non-military ships travelling through the narrow Strait of Gibralter to prevent possible terrorist attacks.[9]

Similar patrol, search and escort activities have been carried out by the US and its allies in the Persian Gulf, the Red Sea and the Arabian Sea. The greater Horn of Africa — an area that includes Sudan, Eritrea, Ethiopia, Somalia, Djibouti, Uganda, Tanzania and Kenya — is a region of interlinked conflicts, weak and failing states, pervasive corruption and extreme poverty. Somalia did not, as feared, become Al-Qaeda's operational base in place of Afghanistan after US-led forces toppled the Taliban regime in 2002 and hunted down its terrorist allies. But Somalia did serve as the base for Al-Qaeda's attacks in Kenya in November 2002 when terrorists in Mombasa detonated a car packed with explosives outside the Paradise Hotel, frequented by Israeli tourists; at least 15 people were killed. At the same time, another group of terrorists shot shoulder-fired missiles at a chartered Israeli jet packed with holidaymakers as it took off from Mombasa's airport, narrowly missing it. The explosives and missiles were reportedly shipped into Kismayo, Somalia, by agents of Al-Qaeda, who had infiltrated parts of coastal Kenya and offshore islands close to Somalia, established a presence, and were able to move back and forth with ease across the porous border of the two countries.[10]

In 2002, to combat terrorism in the greater Horn, the US created the Combined Joint Task Force-Horn of Africa (CJTF-HOA). Some 1,800 US soldiers are allocated to this force, which is backed by the US Central Command. Based in Djibouti, CJTF-HOA's mission is to deter, pre-empt and disable terrorist threats not just from the Horn but from Yemen as well on the other side of the Red Sea and the Gulf of Aden. In June 2003, US President George Bush announced a US$100 million package of counter-terrorism measures to be spent in the greater Horn over 15 months. Half these funds were to support coastal and border security programmes administered by the US Defence Department, US$10 million was to be spent on the Kenyan Anti-terror Police Unit, and US$14 million on Muslim education.[11]

Asia-Pacific Sea Surveillance

The US Pacific Command, based in Hawaii, wants to develop a surveillance arrangement, to be called a comprehensive Regional Maritime Security Program, for Pacific, Southeast Asian and perhaps Indian Ocean waters. The aim is to gain awareness of the maritime domain by extending and expanding knowledge about shipping and its status throughout region.

Such awareness is particularly important in Southeast Asia where the combination of overlapping jurisdictions, thousands of miles of coastlines, and hundreds of remote, jungle-clad islands provide a fertile area for terrorists, pirates and traffickers of drugs and humans to exploit. The US Pacific Fleet commander Admiral Walt Doran, working with other naval chiefs in the region, wants to address these problems in a Southeast Asia Maritime Security programme. The US Pacific Command says that what is needed is an architecture with protocols that provides an accurate tactical picture of the maritime domain, shares real-time information and enables the authorities to counter illicit activities. The US Pacific Command said that Asia-Pacific defence forces have expressed strong interest in the programme and that it is working with the Pentagon and the State Department to make it a reality.[12]

Al-Qaeda's Sea War Plans and Operations

Al-Qaeda has planned and carried out attacks on both military and commercial ships. US officials blame Al-Qaeda for the suicide attack in October 2000 against the American destroyer *USS Cole.* Al-Qaeda was also linked to an earlier aborted plan to carry out a similar attack against another American destroyer, *USS The Sullivans*, in January 2000. Both the *Cole* and *The Sullivans* were in Aden harbour, Yemen, to refuel. The attack against *The Sullivans* failed when the suicide boat, overloaded with explosives, sank. It was salvaged and later used successfully against the *Cole*.[13]

Cole Attack

The two terrorists who attacked the *USS Cole* used a modified dinghy packed with about 500 pounds of C-4 (Composite-4) explosives, nearly sinking one of the US navy's most sophisticated warships. The blast, which which left a 40-foot hole in the side of the destroyer, killed 17 American sailors and wounded 40. It took more than 14 months and cost around US$250 million to repair the ship.[14]

Limburg Attack

The French-registered oil tanker, *Limburg*, carrying crude oil off the coast of Yemen, was crippled and set ablaze in October 2002 in another terrorist attack using an explosive-laden small boat. Al-Qaeda claimed responsibility. The blast ripped through the double-steel hull of the tanker. It stayed afloat and the fire was eventually put out. But one sailor drowned when the crew abandoned the flaming ship. Some 90,000 barrels of oil spilled into the Gulf of Aden.

The *Limburg* was under charter to the Malaysian state petroleum company, Petronas. It had loaded about 400,000 barrels of crude oil in Saudi Arabia, and was planning to load 1.5 million barrels more in Yemen to ship to a refinery in Malaysia, before the attack took place.[15]

Al-Qaeda's Ship Attack Plans

The subsequent capture of a number of terrorist operatives in North Africa, the Persian Gulf and the Horn of Africa, as well as investigations into the attacks on the *USS Cole* and the *Limburg*, uncovered detailed training and planning procedures by Qaeda-linked terrorist networks specifically designed to target maritime interests. Although the arrest of some significant planners and operatives was seen as a setback to Al-Qaeda and its affiliates, the investigations revealed a terrorist network that was larger than previously thought and still capable of carrying out bombings and other attacks against maritime targets.[16]

Al-Qaeda's former chief of naval operations, Abdul Rahim Mohammed Hussein Abda Al-Nasheri, captured in Yemen in November, 2002, gave CIA investigators information that reinforced concerns about plans for terrorist attacks against shipping. Al-Nasheri reportedly admitted playing a key role in organizing the attacks on the *USS Cole* and the *Limburg*. US officials have said that he gave telephone orders to the *Cole* bombers from the United Arab Emirates.[17]

Al-Nasheri, nicknamed the Prince of the Sea, is said to have confessed to planning attacks on shipping in the Strait of Gibralter. Early in 2002, Al-Nashri sent a team of several Afghan-trained Saudis to Morocco to prepare for bomb-laden speedboat attacks on US and British warships as they passed through the Strait between the Mediterranean Sea and the Atlantic Ocean. The Moroccan intelligence service foiled the plot but a key operative escaped.[18]

Al-Nasheri is also suspected of being behind plans to bomb US 5th Fleet Headquarters in Bahrain, a plot revealed in January 2002 by another top Al-Qaeda operative captured in Pakistan after he fled from Afghanistan. The 5th Fleet has responsibility for the Persian Gulf and its vital energy sealanes. It provides ships for the operations of the US Central Command, which was in charge of the war in Afghanistan against the Taliban and Al-Qaeda at the time.

Al-Nasheri — who is said to be a citizen of Saudi Arabia in his thirties — is described as a ruthless professional terrorist. He had been associated with bin Laden since they met in the 1980s when they both went to Afghanistan to fight in the Muslim "holy war" against Soviet forces. Moscow sent troops into Afghanistan in 1979. They were forced out a decade later after suffering heavy losses.[19]

Morocco and Gibraltar

The three citizens of Saudi Arabia captured in Morocco in May and June 2002 in a joint Moroccan-CIA operation reportedly told interrogators that they had escaped from Afghanistan and came to Morocco on a mission to use speedboats packed with explosives for suicide attacks on US and British warships in the Strait of Gibraltar. The Saudis were among a group of Al-Qaeda loyalists, estimated by Western officials to have numbered several hundred, who slipped out of Afghanistan via neighbouring Pakistan after US forces captured Kabul. The US began bombing Afghanistan on 7 October 2001, less than a month after the terrorist attacks on the US, and by the end of November most of the country was in the hands of US forces and their allies.

According to senior Moroccan officials, the three captured Saudis said that, just before leaving Afghanistan, the assembled loyalists were addressed by Al-Nasheri, who said he was carrying direct instructions from bin Laden. Al-Nasheri told them to disperse to whatever areas of the world they had previously operated from, including Asia, the Persian Gulf, Africa, Turkey and Europe. Bin Laden's instruction directed them to launch terrorist attacks once they had become established in familiar areas.

Although some of the loyalists received very general orders, others such as the three Saudis, two of whom were married to Moroccan women, were given specific targets. They were to go to Morocco and attack NATO ships. Britain has a naval repair and supply base in Gibraltar, just 12 miles from Morocco across the Strait of Gibraltar. The strait contains some of the busiest sealanes in the world, through which US navy ships regularly pass.

When captured, the Saudis had US$10,000 between them in cash and had begun inquiring about the purchase of Zodiac-type speedboats. After acquiring the craft, a logistics team, experienced in explosives and weapons, would have come to make them ready for the operation. The Moroccan officials said that the operation bore all the Al-Qaeda hallmarks of slow, careful planning. They also said that the three Saudis were not mere foot soldiers but were educated, ideologically informed and technically proficient in the mechanics of terrorist attacks. The three were each sentenced to ten years in jail by a Moroccan court in February 2003 for plotting to strike Western warships.[20]

There were four major elements in Al-Nasheri's strategy. First, the use of Zodiac-type speedboats loaded with explosives to attack US warships and other targets. Second, the use of medium-sized ships that could be blown up near other vessels, including passenger liners if warships became too difficult to approach. Third, the use of private planes bought or stolen from flying clubs and small airports that could be loaded with explosives and used as suicide bombers against ships. Fourth, training underwater demolition teams to attack vessels.[21]

The Underwater Scare

Shortly after Al-Nasheri was captured in Yemen in November 2002, the FBI issued an alert that terrorists might try to attack shipping, possibly using scuba divers to put explosives on vessels.[22]

In August 2003, the Department of Homeland Security, the US government agency charged with protecting America from terrorist attack, warned that international terrorist groups might be planning to strike from under water.

The Department's bulletin to ship owners, port managers and maritime police organizations said that there were indications that terrorists planned to use scuba divers to hit US ships or ports. Although there was no firm evidence of an actual plot, "there is a body of information showing the desire to obtain such capability". The bulletin said that in the past two years numerous things had happened involving suspicious individuals who were possibly conducting surveillance of port facilities, cruise ship docks, naval bases, dams, bridges and power facilities in the US. There had also been law enforcement reporting of suspicious individuals asking questions to marine shops and schools about equipment and training. The bulletin asked boat and submersible equipment dealers to report any volume purchasing inquiries related to Swimmer Delivery Vehicles (SDVs) and Diver Propulsion Vehicles (DPVs). These are underwater motor-propelled sleds that divers use.

While there was no specific information indicating that a swimmer attack of any kind was being planned in the US, the Department said that "such targeting would be consistent with Al-Qaeda's stated objective to disrupt and undermine vital economic interests in this country and to cause mass casualties and panic".[23]

Anti-terrorist investigators worry that divers trained by Al-Qaeda or its affiliates could plant explosives on the hulls of ships, act as seagoing suicide bombers or sneak aboard vessels and commandeer them for attacks. CIA Director George Tenet told the US Senate Committee on Intelligence in February 2003 that Al-Qaeda was developing new means of striking, including the use of "underwater methods to attack maritime targets".[24]

The Dutch Diving School

Late in 2002, Dutch counter-terrorism agents investigating a possible Al-Qaeda recruitment cell became interested in a scuba school where Kasim Ali, an Iraqi suspected of recruiting terrorists, had become a certified diver and studied to be an instructor. Kasim was one of between 50 and 150 Muslim men who had taken classes with a Tunisian instructor at the school in the city of Eindhoven, about 70 miles southeast of Amsterdam. Many were visiting from North Africa and the Middle East. Two of the world's busiest ports are in

Rotterdam, Netherlands, and Antwerp, Belgium, each a short drive from Eindhoven.

Dutch and US investigators, working together on the case, learned that several of the students in the Eindhoven classes were suspected Islamic extremists. An Algerian, who was certified at the school and later deported by the Dutch, was arrested in France in November 2002 along with an accused terrorist who had escaped from a Dutch jail. A third man, believed to be a Libyan who studied diving in Eindhoven, is being held by authorities in a non-European country because of his ties to extremist violence.

There were also leads linking the diving students with the Al-Qaeda network operatives who were directed by Al-Nasheri to return from Afghanistan to Morocco on a maritime terrorism mission and later convicted in a Moroccan court of plotting attacks on US ships in the Strait of Gibralter.

Underwater Attack

However, professional divers with military experience say that mounting a successful underwater attack against a ship or offshore installation would be more difficult than attacking it with an explosive-laden small boat. Underwater strikes require specialized equipment, training and explosive charges — either limpet mines or waterproof IEDs (improvised explosive devices) that would be attached to the hull of the target vessel. If a terrorist used an Aqua Lung closed-circuit breathing system that does not send tell-tale bubbles to the surface like a Scuba diving system, he would be difficult to detect.

But underwater strikes can be complicated by adverse currents, tides and visibility. With port police approval, a group of professional diving instructors simulated a clandestine underwater approach to a moored cargo ship in Rotterdam harbour. The dark waters and deafening engine noise made it difficult for these experienced divers to manoeuvre. A comparative amateur strapped with heavy explosives — and probably battling stress and fear — would have even more trouble.[25]

Southeast Asia

Omar al-Faruq, Al-Qaeda's head of operations in Southeast Asia who was captured in Indonesia late in 2002 and handed over to the United States, has told interrogators that he planned scuba attacks on US warships in Indonesia. The site chosen was the port of Surabaya, Indonesia's second largest city and the home of an important Indonesian naval base.[26]

The Abu Sayyaf Group in the Philippines — who are known to have had links with Al-Qaeda — kidnapped a maintenance engineer from a holiday resort in the east Malaysian state of Sabah in 2000. On his release in June 2003, the engineer said that his kidnappers knew he was a diving instructor and wanted instruction. Meawhile, the owner of a diving school near the Malaysian capital, Kuala Lumpur, kindled concerns about possible suicide-divers when he said he knew of a number of ethnic Malays who wanted to learn to dive but were strangely uninterested in learning about decompression.[27]

JI and Maritime Terrorism

The Singapore government has said that when it cracked down on the Jemaah Islamiyah network in the island-state starting in December 2001, it discovered that the group had made preliminary plans to prepare for suicide attacks on US warships visiting Singapore. The JI group also intended to carry out multiple ammonium nitrate truck bomb attacks against Western and Israeli diplomatic and other targets in Singapore, including naval bases used by the American military in Singapore, and had started buying the explosives.

The plans to attack US warships with explosive-laden small boats manned by foreign suicide bombers were started in the mid-1990s and were fairly well developed, although never activated. They included a detailed targeting map for a seaborne attack using a small vessel against US ships travelling eastwards from Singapore's Sembawang Wharf via Tekong island. The markings on the map identified a strategic "kill" zone where the channel was narrowest and where the ship would have had no room to avoid a collision with the suicide boat. The plan also took advantage of the geography of the area to hide the attack boat from radar and visual detection until the very last minute. The route and patrol schedule of Singapore's Police Coast Guard in the area had also been monitored.

In early 2001, the plans were revived when two unidentified Middle-Easterners approached Faiz bin Abu Bakar Bafana, the Malaysian JI leader, for information on US mililtary vessels in Singapore. Faiz then instructed members of the JI in Singapore to survey Sembawang Wharf and Changi Naval Base, both of which were being used by visiting American warships. They video-recorded what they observed and a copy of the video was later given to the Middle-Easterners in Kuala Lumpur.[28]

The *Cole* Connection

The planning for the attack on the *USS Cole* in Yemen in October 2000 reportedly began in Malaysia. One of the key suspects — Tafiq Muhammed Saleh bin Roshayd bin Attash, also known as Khallad — is said by US officials to have directed the *Cole* attack with Al-Qaeda maritime commander Al-Nasheri. Attash was plotting another attack on a US ship visiting a Malaysian port in 2000. Less than a year later, Malaysian intelligence foiled a plan to attack a second US ship.[29]

Meanwhile, Attash has been arrested and is now in US custody. He was captured by Pakistani military-intelligence agents in April 2003 in Pakistan's southern port city, Karachi. Five other men were arrested with him, including a nephew of Khalid Shaikh Mohammed. Authorities also seized arms, ammunition, explosives, detonators, transmitters and timer switches.[30]

According to US officials, Attash is also suspected of playing a role in the September 2001 attacks. He met two of the hijackers in the Malaysian capital, Kuala Lumpur, in January 2000. Those terrorists, Khalid al-Mihdhar and Nawaf al-Hazmi, were on the plane that crashed into the US Defense Department in Washington. Attash is believed to have paid for some of the pair's travel before the US attacks.[31]

The Sea Tigers

The Liberation Tigers of Tamil Eelam (LTTE) provide a case study of how terrorist groups can use ships. Indeed, some analysts believe that the Tamil Tigers and Al-Qaeda have learned from each other. They say that the Sri Lankan guerillas trained in Al-Qaeda camps in Afghanistan and that the attack on the *USS Cole* in October 2000 and the French tanker *Limburg* two years later, both near Yemen, copied the LTTE's strikes against shipping. The Sri Lankan government lost at least a dozen naval vessels, both in harbour and at sea, during its long war with the Tamil Tigers who used high-speed boats filled with explosives to ram naval vessels. There have also been reports that members of Jemaah Islamiyah have been trained in the seaborne guerrilla tactics developed by the LTTE.[32]

Founded in 1976, the LTTE is the most powerful group among the Tamil minority in a country with a Sinhalese majority. It used both overt and illegal methods to raise funds, get arms, ammunition and explosives and publicize its cause in fighting since 1983 for a separate state for Tamils in the northeast of the island. The LTTE frequently used suicide bombers in operations against the Sri Lankan government and exploited commercial maritime shipping for years, both to make money and bring in arms, ammunition, and other war-related material for attacks in Sri Lanka. Before Norway brokered a ceasefire between the government and the Tamil Tigers that took effect in February 2002, the LTTE had developed into a prototype terrorist organization with a potentially global reach.[33]

Suicide Attacks

Unlike Al-Qaeda, the Tamil Tigers did not strike extensively outside their home base but had the capability to do so. The LTTE is the only group to have successfully assassinated two national leaders — Rajiv Gandhi of India in 1991 and Ranasinghe Premadasa of Sri Lanka in 1993. Both were well-orchestrated suicide strikes that evaded the tight security cordons of the Indian and Sri Lankan intelligence services. Sri Lanka's current President Chandrika Kumaratunga narrowly survived a Tamil Tiger suicide bomb attack in 1999. She precipitated a political crisis in November 2003 that threatened to undermine the ceasefire after she accused the government of Prime Minister Ranil Wikremesinghe of jeapordizing national security by conceding too much to the LTTE.[34]

Until August 1998, the LTTE had conducted 155 battlefield and civilian suicide attacks, compared to the 50 carried out by all other groups worldwide, including Hamas and Hizbollah in the Middle East, the Kurdish Worker's Party (PKK), in Turkey and the Sikh Babbar Khalsa in South Asia.[35]

The key to the LTTE's fighting strength was its international support network. It collected money from large Tamil communities in North America, Europe and Australia. There is also some evidence, though it is not definitive, that the LTTE officially sanctioned drug smuggling as well as arms smuggling to support its independence struggle.[36]

Tamil Tiger Shipping

Since the mid-1980s, the Tamil Tigers had controlled an extensive and profitable network of freight forwarders and up to a dozen or so cargo ships. The latter were not registered in Sri Lanka. To help disguise their ownership, they flew Panamanian, Honduran or Liberian flags. Indeed, the heart of the LTTE's military procurement was a highly secretive shipping network which, by 1999, included at least ten freighters, all equipped with sophisticated radar and Inmarsat communication technology. Most of the time, the Tamil Tiger ships made money carrying legitimate cargo like timber, tea, rice, cement and fertilizer. But in some cases, the Tamil Tigers are reported to have carried weapons and ammunition for other paying terrorist groups, among them the Harkat-ul-Mujahideen of Pakistan which is a member of the Al-Qaeda-linked International Islamic Front. And when needed, Tamil Tiger ships and traders played a vital role in supplying explosives, weapons, ammunition and other war-related material to the LTTE in Sri Lanka.[37]

In one of the largest such shipments, in August 1994, an LTTE freighter, the *Swene*, loaded 60 tons of RDX and TNT bought from a factory in Ukraine. The transaction was arranged through a Tamil Tiger front company in Dhaka that had produced a forged end-user certificate showing the Bangladesh armed forces as the approved recipient. The shipment was landed on the northeast Sri Lankan coast controlled by the LTTE and transferred to jungle bases. Some of the explosives, between 300 and 400 kilograms, were used in the massive truck-bomb attack against the Central Bank building in Colombo in January 1996 that killed 60 people and injured as many as 1,500.[38]

The Sting

On May 23, 1997, a Greek-registered freighter, the *Stillus Limassul*, left the port Beira in Mozambique for Sri Lanka carrying 32,400 81mm mortar bombs intended for the Sri Lankan army. The deal, worth US$3 million, had been arranged between officials of the Sri Lankan Defence Ministry and the state-owned Zimbabwe Defence Industries. The munitions were shipped by train to Beira. But the Sri Lankan military never received them. This was the result of a well-organized and well-concealed "sting" operation by the LTTE that deeply embarassed the Sri Lankan government at the time.

The Tamil Tigers claimed that on July 11 they had hijacked the *Stillus Limassul* while it was on its way to Colombo. But subsequent investigations revealed that the *Stillus Limassul* was not among the vessels on Lloyds International Shipping Register. It was, in fact, owned by the LTTE itself. Further enquiries uncovered a paper trail that led to Ben Tsoi, an Israeli arms dealer who had arranged the mortar supply and apparently been bribed by the Tamil Tigers to let one of their own freighters collect the consigment. Tsoi's company, LBJ Military Supplies, reportedly persuaded some officials of the Zimbabwe Defence Industries to provide false information to the authorities in Sri Lanka that the shipment had been loaded, as sheduled, in Beira.

LBJ Military Supplies then informed the Sri Lankan government that the munitions were en route, via Walvis Bay, in Namibia, and Madagascar. This gave the LTTE time to complete the sting. By the time Colombo learned the full extent of what had happened, the mortars had been unloaded and trans-shipped by smaller Tamil Tiger vessels to LTTE jungle bases in Sri Lanka. Within weeks, the weapons were being used by the Tamil Tigers to cause serious setbacks to government troops.[39]

External Crackdown

The operating environment for the LTTE outside Sri Lanka has changed since the late 1990s, especially since the US and other countries launched their global campaign against terrorism following the attacks against America in September, 2001. Even if fighting resumes in Sri Lanka's civil war, the LTTE will find it more difficult than before to rebuild its international support and supply lines. Since 1997, a number of countries that were important parts of the network, including the United States, Canada, Britain, India and Australia, have outlawed the Tamil Tigers and sought to disrupt their funding and operations. These countries have made it clear they will only lift the terrorist proscription if the LTTE agrees to negotiated autonomy.

And many of the arms markets and pipelines that the Tamil Tigers once used, among them Pakistan-Afghanistan and Southeast Asia, are now being actively suppressed by governments anxious to support the global war on terrorism and protect themselves from attack.[40]

3 A Maritime Terror Strike — Where and How?

Can Al-Qaeda and its affiliates, including Jemaah Islamiyah (JI), still launch major attacks? Since the terrorist strikes on the US in 2001, many Al-Qaeda leaders have been captured and the organization's financial system, communications networks and training camps in Afghanistan disrupted. Over 3,000 organizers, operatives and supporters in at least 90 countries have been arrested or killed. Since September 11, an informal counter-terrorism coalition of nearly 70 nations has been working together in law enforcement, information-sharing, transportation and cyber security, and financial asset seizure. US officials say that nearly two-thirds of Al-Qaeda's senior leaders, operational managers and key facilitators have been captured or killed, while the rest are on the run.[1]

Southeast Asia

In Southeast Asia, JI has been hounded by tougher law enforcement and better intelligence-sharing among countries in the region and between them and counterpart agencies in the US, Australia and elsewhere. Over 130 JI members have been arrested in five Southeast Asian countries since late 2001, including Hambali, the senior Al-Qaeda operational planner in Southeast Asia.

Yet the JI — described by the Singapore minister in charge of internal security as "Al-Qaeda's closest ally in Southeast Asia" — is said to be planning more terrorist attacks in the region. Both Al-Qaeda and the JI appear to have been able either to maintain an effective command and operational structure or to renew it in a different form.[2]

Networking

Moreover, there is a web of relationships that link the various militant Muslim groups within Southeast Asia and also connect them to

Al-Qaeda. These links were forged over the last two decades, starting with those Southeast Asian Muslims who went to Afghanistan in the 1980s to fight with other mujahidin and who experienced firsthand the glory of jihad and its eventual victory over the Soviet Union. These international connections give the Southeast Asian militants greater reach and resilience.

The militants include hardline elements in the separatist Moro Islamic Liberation Front (MILF) in the Philippines, and a small breakaway faction of Filipino Muslim separatists, the Abu Sayyaf Group, which kidnaps for ransom. Al-Qaeda provided funds and training to the Abu Sayyaf and the much larger MILF through a network of front organizations and legitimate Muslim bodies. Al-Qaeda forged similar links with several militant Islamic groups in Indonesia in addition to the JI which has members spread over Southeast Asia. Extremist factions in the MILF have for years provided training grounds and protection on Mindanao island in the southern Philippines for JI members from elsewhere in the region. And they continue to do so, despite denials by MILF leaders.[3]

Al-Qaeda is regarded by Western and Asian officials as being less capable than before of striking at American embassies, military targets and landmarks that were the hallmarks of its campaign until the September 2001 attacks in the US. But the terrorist threat has evolved into a much broader, more diffuse, phenomenon, with a new strategy of attacks by loosely affiliated groups against highly vulnerable targets. Such strikes are even more difficult to guard against. There is also deep concern in the US, Europe and Asia that they are facing more — not fewer — terrorist foes than before. The killing and capturing of Al-Qaeda leaders is failing to keep pace with the number of angry young Muslim men and women willing to participate in suicide attacks.[4]

Franchising

Al-Qaeda's hands-on leadership role in terrorist attacks has diminished since the campaign against international terrorism was intensified. But the organization has successfully franchised its brand of synchronized, devastating violence and suicide bombing to homegrown terrorist groups across the world, posing a formidable new challenge to counter-terrorism forces. This worries many governments.[5]

Attacks in 2003 in Turkey, Indonesia, Morocco, Saudi Arabia, Chechnya and Iraq show that the smaller groups, most of whose leaders were trained in Al-Qaeda camps in Afghanistan, have fanned out, imbued with radical ideology and the means to create or revitalize local terrorist groups. The main link among the groups appears to be their shared experiences in the Al-Qaeda training camps in Afghanistan. As many as 20,000 people from 47 countries passed through the camps from 1996, when bin Laden returned to Afghanistan from Sudan, until the US-led invasion of Afghanistan in October 2001. The camps served as a place where fighters were trained and indoctrinated, keys to building the future network as they returned to their homelands. The camps were also a place to make religious and ideological contacts.[6]

Militants who trained in Afghanistan have returned to Indonesia, Malaysia, the Philippines, Turkey, Morocco, Saudi Arabia, Turkey, Chechnya and other countries in Asia, Europe and the Middle East, possibly including Iraq. The US and Canada have also arrested men allegedly trained in the Afghan camps. Some Australians and Britons, too, have undergone the training. As extremists graduated, they either pledged their allegiance to bin Laden and Al-Qaeda or carried his message and inspiration back to their home countries to initiate more localized jihad, or holy war, efforts. Those who were trained are now training the next generation of terrorists. The terrorist exodus from Afghanistan has created a diaspora of destruction that the world is today struggling to contain.[7]

This religious and ideological bonding provides the glue for Al-Qaeda's international reach. Al-Qaeda-style terrorism is new and unique because it is global. There is a shared fanatical zealousness among these different extremists around the world.[8]

The Ideology of Terror

Al-Qaeda as an ideology is now stronger than Al-Qaeda as an organization. As a result, terrorists influenced by Al-Qaeda launch more frequent attacks on varied targets, many of them so-called soft targets like synagogues, churches, hotels, nightclubs, banks and public transport. The presence of US, British, Australian and other foreign forces and agencies in Iraq is being used by extremist Muslim leaders rally their followers to jihad, or holy war, around the world. The very name Al-Qaeda has become shorthand for a larger jihad fed by the Iraq war and Israeli-Palestinian conflict.

The resurgent global menace leads critics to assert that the US-led military operations in Afghanistan and Iraq have boomeranged by scattering Al-Qaeda's forces, making them harder to detect, and inspiring like-minded extremists. Yet some US and European officials see signs of weakness as inexperienced terrorists turn to soft targets.[9]

The terrorist bombings in Turkey in November 2003, like earlier attacks in Southeast Asia, are part of the new pattern of international terrorism, with Al-Qaeda using local groups as proxies in its global network of connections. Al-Qaeda is using local terrorist organizations to carry out attacks in Asia, Africa, the Middle East and parts of Europe such as Spain, Britain and Chechnya.[10]

Where Now?

In summary, many Al-Qaeda leaders have been captured and the organization's financial system, communications networks and training camps in Afghanistan disrupted, since the terrorist attacks on the US in 2001. In Southeast Asia, Al-Qaeda's closest ally, the JI, has also been hounded by tougher law enforcement and better intelligence-sharing among countries in the region and between them and counterpart agencies in the US, Australia and elsewhere. In addition, many new security measures to protect maritime trade, container cargo shipments and their land connections in the global supply chain have been implemented or will be during 2004.

How will this affect the plans for maritime-related terrorism that Al-Qaeda and its affiliates, including the JI in Southeast Asia, were trying to develop and implement? Al-Qaeda clearly had a much more sophisticated programme for striking at seaborne trade and the global cargo container supply chain than JI, which so far as is publicly known had only prepared a preliminary plan to attack US warships in or close to Singapore.

The operational capability of both Al-Qaeda and JI have certainly been set back. But, given the protean nature of the Al-Qaeda network, no one can be sure how serious a blow has been struck or how long the terrorists will take to recover and attack again. Their fight is likely to continue for a long time and take many different forms.

The capture of dozens of terrorist operatives in 2002 and 2003 in North Africa, the Persian Gulf, the Horn of Africa and Pakistan, as well as investigations into the attacks on the *USS Cole* and the *Limburg*, uncovered detailed training and planning procedures by Al-Qaeda-linked terrorist networks specifically designed to target maritime interests. Although the arrest of some significant planners and operatives was seen as a setback to Al-Qaeda and its affiliates, the investigations revealed a terrorist network that is larger than previously thought and still capable of carrying out bombings and other attacks against maritime targets.

The Big Bang

Moreover, building and detonating a radiological bomb or commandeering ships and using them as weapons to attack key port-cities, straits or waterways are well within the capability of Al-Qaeda and some of its affiliates. So constant vigilance must be maintained and layered defences built to guard against such attacks.[11]

Many officials and security experts fear that Al-Qaeda-linked terrorists aim to:

- sink, set alight or explode a huge tanker laden with inflammable material in a key port, strait, canal or internal waterway for international shipping, or
- pack a ship with explosives, sail it into the harbour of a leading port-city and detonate it there to cause maximum casualties, destruction and panic.

Where and how might well-organized terrorists strike against the seaborne trading system or its land-links in the global supply chain?

Bombing attacks against individual vessels have been the only method planned and carried out so far. But the frequency of pirate attacks, particularly in Southeast Asian waters, has shown that ships are vulnerable to boarding and seizure by armed raiders, including, potentially, by terrorist groups.

Aegis

A study published in October 2003 by Aegis Defence Services, a security consultancy based in London, reported what it said were several new and disturbing developments for maritime terrorism in Southeast Asia. In March 2003, the chemical tanker *Dewi Madrim* was boarded off the coast of Sumatra in Indonesian waters by ten pirates from a speedboat. They were armed with machine guns and machetes and carried VHF (very high frequency) radios. They disabled the ship's radio, took the helm and steered the vessel, altering speed, for about an hour. Then they left, with some cash and the captain and first officer, who are still missing.

The Aegis report concluded that this was a case of terrorists learning to drive a ship, and that the kidnapping (without any attempt to ransom the officers) was designed to acquire expertise for carrying out a maritime attack. The *Economist* described the takeover of the

Dewi Madrim as "the equivalent of the Al-Qaeda hijackers who perpetrated the September 11 attacks going to flying school in Florida." However, the International Maritime Bureau says that its Piracy Reporting Centre in Kuala Lumpur has received confirmation from the owners of the *Dewi Madrim* that the attack was not as described by Aegis. It was, in fact, a criminal operation to steal money and valuables and none of the crew members were abducted.[12]

The Aegis report also identified ten cases of Southeast Asian pirates stealing tugs for no apparent reason. The worry is that they are for use to tow a hijacked laden super-tanker into a busy international port, such as Singapore, or the Malacca and Singapore Straits and scuttle it to create a major blockage and oil spil, or blow it up to start a massive blaze.[13]

Taking Over a Ship

How could terrorists take control of a ship? Would they collaborate with pirates or criminal gangs involved in the robbery or hijacking of vessels? In 2003, the International Maritime Bureau, an arm of the International Chamber of Commerce, named Indonesia's waters adjacent to the Malacca/Singapore Straits as the most dangerous on the planet, accounting for 87 of the world's 344 pirate attacks in the first 9 months of the year.

But it is more likely that Al-Qaeda would use its own ships, or its own agents to take control of a vessel, for a major maritime terrorist attack. This would give the organization better control over any operation. Otherwise it would have to rely on people from outside its circle of zealots, whom it might not be able to trust. Moreover, for pirates, and any criminal syndicates behind them, a serious terrorist attack would be bad for business-as-usual because it would almost certainly lead to a crackdown that would make future sea robberies more difficult.

Seafarers and Sleepers

Al-Qaida and its international affiliates could, with relative ease, infiltrate the ranks of over 1.2 million seafarers, most of them sourced from Asia, Eastern Europe and Russia. The main supply countries are the Philippines, Indonesia, Russia, Ukraine, Poland, China, India, Greece, South Korea, Croatia and Romania. Over 400,000 of these seafarers are officers while more than 800,000 are ratings.[14]

There is intense competition for employment on ships because wages are relatively high for many seafarers as a result of hard bargaining over many years by the the International Transport

Workers' Federation (ITF) and its affiliated unions. In late 2003, the worldwide benchmark for a deckhand was US$1,300 per month — much more than many seafarers from Asia, Eastern Europe and Russia could expect to earn in their home countries.[15]

Fake Certificates

Demand for seafaring jobs exceeds supply. Regulation of recruitment and manning practices is lax. As a result, fraud and corruption are rife. Research in the past few years has shown that a large number of certificates held by seafarers are fraudulent and that fake papers for crew members can be bought and sold easily. Late in 1999, the International Maritime Organisation (IMO) asked the Seafarers International Research Centre (SIRC) at Cardiff University in Wales, Britain, to investigate the nature and extent of illegal practices associated with certificates of competency issued to seafarers. The report to the IMO in June 2001 concluded that fraudulent certificates, used by seafarers to get jobs on ships, were widespread. In all, 82 per cent of the the respondents in the SIRC survey had detected forged certificates of competency in the last five years.

The SIRC researchers visited countries in South and Southeast Asia, Eastern Europe and Latin America that were either labour suppliers to the international fleet or operated large registers for ships. They reported that measures to prevent and penalize fraudulent practices existed in most of the countries surveyed but implementation of these measures was frequently ineffective. Their report said that in 10 of the 13 countries visited, it was evident that forgery was more than a backroom business. "It was typically well-organised with effective linkages into maritime administrations, employers, manning agents and training establishments. In several cases, forgers operated transnationally."[16]

Reputable shipowners take care in recruiting officers and crew. They run background security checks on those they hire. But a significant proportion of the world's commercial fleet gets crews from manning agencies which are supposed to match candidates with the requirements of ship owners and operators. While many of these agencies ensure that the seafarers they represent fulfil international requirements and pass background checks, some do not.[17]

Peter Morris, a former Australian transport minister who chairs the International Commission on Shipping which published its report "Ships, Slaves and Competition" in March 2001, says that some of the many private manning agencies that compete for business in developing countries are involved in the secret and illegal recruitment and transfer of people posing as seafarers to other countries, in many cases after providing them with forged and unearned qualification certificates. He says that certification fraud breaches ship security and underlines the need to authenticate the identity of seafarers.[18]

In 2001, the ITF reported that it had bought a First Officer's certificate for its General Secretary, David Cockroft, who is a "landlubber" with no shipboard training or experience, from Panama which operates the world's largest ship register. The ITF said it paid US$4,500 for the certificate and seaman's book that authorized Cockroft to navigate a vessel and deputize for its captain, despite his complete lack of marine qualifications and skills. The ITF says it is disappointed with progress since 2001 to tighten up certification of seafarers. There have been few responses to an IMO circular requesting reports from member states on fraudulent certificates found and prosecutions made. And the ITF says that, as of mid-2003, fake certificates continue to be issued.

In such a situation, there is considerable scope for terrorists to pose as crew and then take over a ship to use it as a weapon of attack. Many large modern ships are highly automated and can be operated by crews of well under 20 officers and ratings. So it would only take a small number of well-trained and determined terrorists to seize command of a big ship.[19]

Biometric IDs

In a move to guard against terrorists infiltrating the ranks of the world's 1.2 million seafarers, the International Labour Organization (ILO) adopted a convention in June 2003 for a new seafarer identification document (ID) with a biometric imprint. This is an electronic recording of a person's unique physical characteristic, usually a thumb or eye retina print, that allows immigration authorities to use a scanner or computer to match the ID with its bearer. The aim is to get a universal ID card for seafarers that will be identical throughout the world, easy to verify in a scan and hard to forge.

The US had already tightened its entry requirements for foreign seafarers. Seafarers have traditionally been granted relatively liberal landing and travel rights by governments when they present their seafarer identity documents. But since September 11, the Bush administration has imposed restrictions on seafarer movement in the US, arguing that they must be monitored more closely.

Under the ILO convention, governments are to issue the new ID cards to their seafarer nationals and permanent residents. Possession of a valid ID card is intended to allow seafarers to disembark from ships in a foreign port for shore leave, transit to another country, transfer to another vessel or repatriation unless there are pressing security reasons for not doing so or clear grounds for doubting the authenticity of the bearer's ID.[20]

However, some critics say that biometric technology is far from foolproof and that while it can improve security in some situations, its costs often outweigh its benefits. Even the most advanced systems falsely reject a small proportion of legitimate users, and falsely accept illegitimate ones. Both the US and Europe plan to start issuing biometric passports as early as 2004, while biometric national ID cards are being adopted in a number of countries in Asia, Europe and the Middle East. Critics assert that biometrics seem to be attractive to politicians because the technology, long familiar from science fiction and spy films, gives the impression that something dramatic is being done to improve security. Moreover, a widespread system of biometric seafarer IDs would not necessarily unmask terrorists who managed to get and carry them.[21]

Chokepoints in Maritime Trade

Al-Qaeda and affiliated terrorist organizations, including the JI in Southeast Asia, have shown that they understand the role of major chokepoints in global seaborne trade by the maritime attacks they have mounted or planned in the past few years. The results of two of the attacks close to Yemen, on the *USS Cole* in October 2000 and the *Limburg* in October 2002, were dramatic but largely localized. Insurance rates shot up and ships avoided the area.

As noted in Chapter 1, most international trade — about 80 per cent of the total by volume — is carried by sea. World maritime trade set a record in 2002, reaching almost 5.9 billion metric tons. A further significant rise is expected in 2003.[22]

Sixty per cent of the world's oil supply is transported by approximately 3,500 oceangoing tankers. These range in size from Ultra Large Crude Carriers (ULCCs) of more than 300,000 dead weight tons (dwt) and Very Large Crude Carriers (VLCCs) of between 200,000 and 300,000 dwt, to Handymax tankers of around 35,000 dwt and smaller Handy Size tankers of between 20,000 and 30,000 dwt.

Seventy-five per cent of global maritime trade passes through a handful of relatively narrow shipping lanes. Nearly 35 million barrels of oil per day — just under half the world's daily consumption of nearly 78 million barrels in 2002 — passes through six geographic "chokepoints", or narrow channels. An increasing proportion of the global trade in liquified natural gas, or LNG, is carried through some of the same channels.

These channels are critically important to the world's trade because so much of it passes through them. Yet they are also "chokepoints" because they are narrow enough to be blocked, at least temporarily, by an accident or by an attack, including a terrorist operation.[23]

Many of the vessels that pass through these straits and canals are laden supertankers, or carriers of LNG or liquified petroleum gas (LPG), chemicals and other inflammable, explosive or dangerous material that could be attractive to terrorists as floating bombs or major sources of pollution. Oil tankers and dry bulk carriers together make up almost 72 per cent of the total world commercial shipping fleet by tonnage. According to the International Association of Independent Tanker Owners (Intertanko), tankers carry close to 40 per cent of global seaborne trade.[24]

Very large crude carriers, or VLCCs, typically carry over 2 million barrels of oil on every voyage. They are huge and slow, with a cruising speed of some 15 knots. And they are a common sight; about 3,000 big tankers ply the world's shipping lanes.[25]

Hormuz Strait

Nearly half the world's oil flows through this short strait, which is less than 40 nautical miles across from Iran on one side and Oman on the other. The Middle East, mainly the Persian Gulf, accounts for over 65 per cent of the world's proven oil reserves and 36 per cent of its proven gas reserves. Japan, South Korea and, increasingly, China are critically dependent on the Gulf energy supplies that pass through the Hormuz Strait; the US and Western Europe are much less reliant on Gulf oil, but still regard it as a key strategic chokepoint.

The strait consists of 2-mile wide channels for separate inbound and outbound tanker traffic, as well as a 2-mile wide buffer zone between them. Closure of the strait to the estimated 13 million barrels of oil per day that passed through it in 2002, would require use of longer alternative oil export routes at a higher cost. Assuming space was available, such routes include five overland export pipelines from the Gulf with a capacity of at least 7.4 million barrels per day.

Such a shutdown would be a severe strategic shock for Northeast Asia, North America and Western Europe, even if it did not last for long. This is why the US and its allies attach such importance to freedom of navigation through the strait. They protect it with regular warship patrols, and station naval vessels in the Gulf.[26]

Malacca and Singapore Straits

About a quarter of the world's trade, half its oil pass and much of its LNG pass through this waterway between the islands of Indonesia to the south, and peninsular Malaysia and Singapore to the north. Most of the oil imported by Japan, South Korea and China comes from the Persian Gulf via the Malacca and Singapore Straits.[27]

Although over 600 miles long, the straits are congested and only 1.5 miles wide at their narrowest point in the Phillips channel near Singapore, the world's busiest port, with a population of four million. As many as 50,000 large ships use the waterway each year.

In 2002, an average of 45 tankers a day, carrying over 10 million barrels of oil, passed through the Malacca and Singapore Straits, a number projected to rise to nearly 60 per day by 2010 as Northeast Asian demand, especially from China, for imported oil from the Persian Gulf rises. In the same period, the number of LNG carriers using the straits each day is forecast to increase from 8 to 12, and the number of LPG carriers from 5 to 7. This can only increase the strategic importance of this vital sealane in future.[28]

There are two alternative waterways for international shipping through the Indonesian islands that could be used if the Malacca and Singapore Straits were closed — the Sunda Strait and the Lombok and Makassar Straits. Both are deepwater channels. But even a detour through the Sunda Strait, the shortest alternative between the Persian Gulf and Northeast Asian energy consumers, would add a significant amount of time, and therefore cost, to the voyage. Moreover, a sealane disruption simulation exercise conducted in April 2003 by the Tokyo-based Asia Pacific Energy Research Centre highlighted the inadequacy of navigational aids in both the Sunda and Lombok straits should a shipping crisis block the Malacca and Singapore Straits.

There is a draft limit in the Malacca and Singapore Straits. They are 25 metres deep at their shallowest point. Ships using them require an under-keel clearance of 3.5 metres to comply with navigation rules issued by the International Maritime Organization (IMO) the United Nations agency responsible for regulating global shipping. Laden oil tankers over about 250,000 tons are probably outside these draft limits and would normally use the Lombok and Makassar Straits, although this might add about 1,000 nautical miles and three days' steaming to the passage between the Persian Gulf and ports in Northeast Asia.

Indeed, the US Department of Energy has calculated that if the Malacca and Singapore Straits were closed, nearly half the world's fleet would have to sail further, generating a substantial rise in the requirement for vessel capacity, largely because of China's rapidly growing export-import trade. If this were to happen today, when demand for ships is exceeding supply, shipbuilding costs would rise.

Closure of the Malacca and Singapore Straits would also increase freight rates worldwide. It would jolt the economies of China, Japan, South Korea and Taiwan, which rely on imported energy for continued growth. If the closure lasted for long, it could also be disastrous for Singapore's economy. Singapore is the 19th biggest trading nation and one of the world's most trade-dependent countries. The value of its trade is three times its GDP. At any one time, an average of 800 ships and 150,000 three times containers are in Singapore's port.

The terrorist bombings against land targets in Indonesia since October 2002 have raised concerns that extremist groups in Southeast Asia affiliated to Al-Qaeda could try to stage a major operation in the Malacca and Singapore Straits.

Of all the major international straits, the Malacca and Singapore Straits are the most vulnerable to attack and the easiest for a terrorist group to block, with the possible exception of the Bosporus and Turkish Straits. But the Malacca and Singapore Straits are far more vital to global seaborne trade than the straits that bisect Turkey. The closure of this key waterway in Southeast Asia would disrupt world commerce, although its impact would not be as catastrophic as a nuclear or radiological bomb attack on a mega port-city.[29]

Panama Canal

This 50-mile waterway through Panama links the Pacific Ocean with the Caribbean Sea and Atlantic Ocean. It has a number of narrow locks. The largest tanker that can use the Panama Canal is the

Panamax class of around 50,000 deadweight tons. Only about 600,000 barrels of oil per day passes through the canal and only a small portion of the crude oil and refined products imported into the US comes this way.

If transit were halted through the canal, the Trans-Panama pipeline could be reopened to carry oil in either direction. It has a capacity of 860,000 barrels of oil per day. Much of Asia's container trade with the centre and east coast of the US goes in and out via west coast ports. Trains and trucks haul the boxes overland.

Suez Canal

Connecting the Red Sea and Gulf of Suez with the Mediterranean Sea, this busy international shipping canal carries around 1.3 million barrels of oil per day. The biggest tankers it can currently accommodate are the Suezmax class of between 125,000 and 180,000 deadweight tons. The Egyptian government plans to widen and deepen the Suez Canal so that by 2010 it can take laden tankers of more than 300,000 deadweight tons.

Bab el-Mandab passage

As much as 3.3 million barrels of oil per day is estimated to pass in tankers through this passage between Djibouti and Eritrea on the Horn of Africa and Yemen in the southwest of the Arabian peninsula. US forces are based in Djibouti to hunt for terrorists and ensure that the passage remains open.

The *Limburg*, a Very Large Crude Carrier (VLCC) laden with 400,000 barrels of oil, that was set ablaze in a terrorist bombing off the coast of Yemen in October 2002, was not far from the Bab el-Mandab. Closure of the passage could keep tankers from the Persian Gulf from reaching the Suez Canal/Sumed pipeline complex. Instead, they would have to divert around the Cape of Good Hope on the southern tip of Africa. This would add greatly to transit time and cost for oil going to North America and Europe. It would also tie up spare tanker capacity.

For northbound traffic, the Bab el-Mandab could be bypassed by using the East-West oil pipeline that crosses Saudi Arabia and has a capacity of about 4.8 million barrels of oil per day, assuming the pipeline could carry the extra load. But southbound oil traffic would still be blocked. In addition, closure of the Bab el-Mandab would block non-oil shipping from using the Suez Canal, except for limited trade within the Red Sea region.[30]

Bosporus and Turkish Straits

This 17-mile long waterway connecting the Black Sea with the Mediterranean Sea divides Asia from Europe and is just half a mile wide at its narrowest point. The straits are the only southern shipping route for oil and commodities from Russia and the energy-rich Caspian Sea. The Black Sea is the largest outlet for Russian oil exports. Two-and-a-half million barrels a day of crude oil and refined products and 140 ships pass through the Bosporus each day, or 50,000 vessels a year, the same number as use the Malacca and Singapore Straits. Of these, up to 8,000 carry oil or other potentially hazardous cargo.

Congestion is common, and the Bosporus/Turkish straits have often been closed following bad weather or accidents. Istanbul, a city of 10 million people, straddles the waterway. Citing safety concerns, Turkey has imposed restrictions on Bosporus traffic. Since October 2002, it has banned the passage of ships longer than 200 metres at night. Ships carrying dangerous cargo, including oil, must request permission to transit 48 hours in advance. Restrictions have also been imposed on large LNG and LPG carriers.

Two huge truck bombs outside the British consulate and the British-based HSBC banking group killed more than 25 people in Istanbul in November 2003, just five days after the bombing of two synagogues in the city left 25 dead. Turkish prosecutors allege that the strikes by Islamic militants were ordered by Al-Qaeda. After the attacks, some analysts warned that the Bosporus could be a tempting target for Al-Qaeda, although they saw no signs of a specific threat.[31]

Ships as Weapons

Among the vessels that could be used by terrorists to block or disrupt critical straits, waterways and port-cities are big ships carrying crude oil, especially fuel and other heavy oils, toxic chemicals, petrol, ammonium nitrate, liquified petroleum gas and liquified natural gas.

Large modern oil tankers have double steel hulls, for added protection in case of rough weather, collision or grounding. The attack on the *Limburg*, using an explosive-laden small boat, breached the double-hull and caused a fire that took many hours to extinguish. The blast and the blaze severely damaged the tanker, and nearly a quarter of its 400,000 barrels of crude oil spilled into the sea. But the ship did not sink. Nor was it in a vital waterway for international shipping, although it was not far from the Bab el-Mandab Strait at the entrance to the Red Sea.

Terrorists could mount an external attack on a large laden tanker and sink it in the narrowest part of a vital waterway for international shipping, such as the Straits of Malacca and Singapore or the Bosporus and Turkish Straits. Perhaps more likely, terrorists could commandeer the vessel by posing as crew and then ground, sink or set it ablaze, spilling the oil and causing a major danger to shipping as well as an environmental disaster.

Tanker Accidents

Since 1979, there have been at least 17 major tanker accidents around the world, with four of them each involving well over 200,000 metric tons of oil. But some of the most damaging sinkings, groundings or collisions have been the result of smaller releases of heavy oils. Heavy fuel oil, for example, is a common tanker cargo. It will not disperse or emulsify easily when treated with detergents to clean up a spill. And it tends to stick to the seafloor, resulting in the long-term contamination of shellfish beds and the closure of parts of fisheries around inlets where a lot of oil has settled.

Over half the world's 10,000 tankers are old-style vessels with single hulls. When one of them, the *Prestige*, broke in two in a winter storm in November 2002 and sank about 245 kilometres off the northwest coast of Spain, spilling much of its 63,000 tons of heavy fuel oil into the sea, it fouled the Spanish coastline for months afterwards, creating a costly environmental disaster.[32]

Prestige Effect

The *Prestige* sinking galvanized Europe's political leadership to take tough action. In October 2003, the European Union banned single hull tankers from the ports, offshore installations and waters of its 15 member states if they were carrying heavy grades of oil.

Europe's strong-arm tactics prompted the IMO to agree in December 2003 to bring forward its deadline for phasing out single hull tankers by five years, to 2010, for most vessels. The IMO also agreed that from 2005, heavy oils can only be carried in double hull tankers of 5,000 deadweight tons and above. Smaller single hull tankers that do not generally make long sea voyages can carry heavy oils until 2008.

As a result, there are now glaring inconsistencies between EU and international rules for the tanker trade. This will push more single hull vessels towards Asia, where demand for imported oil is strongest. They will become even more heavily engaged in carrying oil through the Southeast Asian straits to Northeast Asia — to Japan, South Korea, Taiwan and China. The breakneck pace of China's economic expansion is leading to a huge surge in oil imports and China is expected to overtake Japan as Asia's biggest oil consumer in 2004.[33]

Of course, not all old tankers with single hulls are unsafe. But there have been some near-disasters from tanker collisions in Asian waters in recent years. For example, in December 2002, just a month after the *Prestige* went down off Spain, a single hull tanker collided with a cargo ship at the eastern entrance to the Malacca and Singapore Straits. Fortunately, the tanker sustained relatively minor damage and only about 350 tons of its 86,000 tons of crude oil spilled into the sea.[34]

The migration of single hull tankers to Asia before they are phased out by 2010 under the IMO's global rules will increase the risk of a major oil spill — possibly one engineered by terrorists.

LNG and LPG Carriers

What would happen if terrorists tried to blow up an LNG or LPG carrier, or set it ablaze? The question worries some officials in the US, Europe and Asia. One of the first maritime-related security actions taken after Al-Qaeda used the US aviation system to attack New York and Washington in September 2001 was to ban entry to a shipment of LNG into Boston harbour until the authorities considered it was safe.[35]

However, a considerable body of evidence suggests that LNG or LPG carriers may not be as vulnerable or as tempting a target as other big ships that carry crude oil, especially fuel and other heavy oils, toxic chemicals, petrol and ammonium nitrate. For example, a fire in November 2002 aboard the LPG tanker *Gaz Poem* failed to ignite the partially laden tanks, while a direct hit on a laden LNG carrier by an Exocet missile during the Iran-Iraq war in the 1980s did not cause an explosion. The main risk from LPG and LNG is during loading or unloading when the cargo can be released in a gaseous state.[36]

LNG

Natural gas is about 90 per cent methane and when it is cooled to minus 161.5 degrees Celsius (256 degrees Fahrenheit) it concentrates into liquid, hence the term liquified natural gas. During the refrigeration process, elements that would make natural gas explosive, like oxygen and hydrocarbons such as propane, ethane and butane, are removed as they freeze when the gas is supercooled. LNG is not stored under pressure and will not explode. But at certain concentrations — when the liquid is returning to its gaseous form — the fuel is highly flammable. LNG will burn only if it escapes or is released into the atmosphere and mixes with air in a 5 to 15 per cent gas-to-air ratio and there has to be a source of ignition.

LNG is 600 times smaller in volume than natural gas and can be transported long distances by tankers. There are over 130 LNG carriers in service and more are being built as demand for the fuel increases rapidly in the United States, Europe and Asia. These tankers are among the strongest and most technologically advanced ships in the world and, since the terrorist attacks on the US in September 2001, they are closely guarded as they approach their receiving and regasification terminals in LNG importing countries. LNG carriers have double hulls and double-walled, insulated cargo storage tanks to guard against leaks and keep the LNG cold. The tanks are, in effect, giant reinforced thermos flasks. A typical LNG tanker contains as many as five tanks with a combined capacity of some 33 million gallons of LNG — enough to heat 30,000 homes for a year. The ships are up to 1,000-feet long, or the length of three football fields.[37]

From 1952 until 2003, LNG ships made more than 33,000 voyages worldwide, carrying over three billion cubic meters of the fuel. Accidents have included engine room fires, serious collisions with other vessels, and eight cases of cargo spillage. But there have been no LNG explosions or fires following these accidents. Still, there remains some concern about a possible terrorist attack on an LNG carrier or loading/unloading facility, possibly using a powerful explosive charge or a stand-off weapon such as an RPG (rocket-propelled grenade). An ignited LNG vapour cloud would be very dangerous, because of its tremendous radiant heat output. As it burned, the flame could spread back towards the evaporating pool of liquid. A fire of this kind could cause extensive damage to life and property, especially if it was near a city or work place.

Spilled LNG would disperse faster on the ocean than on land. LNG also vaporizes more quickly on water because the ocean provides a relatively enormous heat source. For these reasons, most analysts conclude that the risks associated with shipping, loading and offloading LNG are much greater than those associated with land-based LNG storage facilities.[38]

Ammonium Nitrate

Ammonium nitrate is used as an agricultural fertilizer throughout the world. It is widely, and legally, available. For example, the US and other OECD countries imported over 1.6 million tons of ammonium nitrate in 2000 — mostly by sea. As a commercial-grade explosive, it is often used for blasting in construction projects and in mining.

But ammonium nitrate is also of special interest to terrorists because it can be acquired quite easily in many places and then can be made into a powerful explosive when mixed with fuel oil by a bombmaker. It was used in frequent IRA car bombings. It was also the main explosive in the terrorist truck bombings in Oklahoma city in 1995, against the US embassies in Nairobi, Kenya, and in Dar es Salaam, Tanzania, in 1998, as well as in Al-Qaeda's first attempt to attack the World Trade Center in 1993. Turkish police say that ammonium-nitrate explosives were used in four deadly suicide truck bombings in Istanbul in November 2003 that killed 61 people, including the four suicide bombers, and wounded 712. Turkish prosecutors allege that the strikes by Islamic militants were ordered by Al-Qaeda. The US blames Al-Qaeda for the 1998 bombings against its embassies in East Africa.[39]

Ammonium nitrate was used in the van bombing outside the Marriott Hotel in Jakarta in August, 2003. Indonesia produces or imports more than 100,000 metric tons of explosive material, including ammonium nitrate, each year. Indonesian defence officials say that controlling this material is difficult because there are many firms with production and distribution permits. They want a special monitoring agency to be established. Up to 10,000 tons of Indonesia's total supply of explosive materials may "disappear" every year. Rampant illegal mining and fish-bombing contribute to the problem.[40]

Baltic Sky

In June 2003, Greek commandos boarded a cargo ship that had been zig-zagging around the Mediterranean Sea for nearly six weeks in a way that arroused suspicion. The *Baltic Sky* was found to be packed with 680 metric tons of ammonium nitrate-based explosive and 8,000 detonators. The ship's manifest said that the cargo was loaded in Tunisia bound for a company in Sudan. But the Greek Shipping

Minister Giorgos Anomeritis said that the company, identified as Integrated Chemicals and Development, was just "a post office box in Khartoum that did not exist".

The Tunisian firm that had manufactured the explosives filed a complaint against the Baltic Sky, alleging that it had failed to fulfil a contract to deliver the cargo, intended for civilian use, to Sudan. It accused the captain and crew of diverting from their original route and threatening not to deliver the cargo to its rightful destination. The freighter apparently never headed toward the Suez Canal, the direction that would bring it to Sudan.

Greek officials said that the *Baltic Sky* flew the flag of the Comoros Islands, a country in the Indian Ocean off the southeast coast of Africa between Madagascar and Mozambique, until shortly before its detention. The Comoros is used by shipping companies as a flag of convenience to avoid taxes and regulation and guarantee anonymity and freedom from prosecution for the owner. The Comoros shipping register opened for business in late 2000 or early 2001 and branded itself as the world's first Islamic flag of convenience. Its office in Greece, known as the Shipping Activities Bureau, also marketed the North Korean flag.

The *Baltic Sky* was previously called the *Sea Runner* and flew a Cambodian flag. Its 37-year life in the shipping industry was marked by frequent changes of owner and flag, and frequent brushes with the law. It was boarded as part of the international war on terror and had been tracked by Greece and other NATO countries before it was seized and forced to dock, for safety reasons, in a remote Greek harbour.

Greek authorities said that when the *Baltic Sky* was intercepted in Greek territorial waters it was not flying a flag and could therefore be detained. The freighter's captain and crew were charged with illegal possession and transport of explosives. Anomeritis said the authorities were looking into various possibilities: that it was a terrorist shipment; a legitimate business deal that fell apart; or that its crew simply got cold feet delivering dangerous cargo with US-led anti-terrorist efforts in full swing around Sudan and the Horn of Africa region.

The Greek merchant marine ministry said that the *Baltic Sky*'s cargo was "the biggest quantity of explosives ever seized in the world from a ship sailing illegally". Anomeritis described the ship's potential explosive power as akin to "an atomic bomb". This was an exaggeration but it certainly would have wreaked havoc had it been detonated near a port-city.[41]

Texas City

On April 16 and 17, 1947, the port of Texas City on the Gulf of Mexico was devastated when two ships containing ammonium nitrate exploded in what was one of the worst industrial disasters in US history. Ammonium nitrate is a crystalline powder that is an excellent peacetime source of nitrogen for crops. In World War II, the substance was combined with TNT to make a bursting charge in demolition bombs.

The French-owned cargo ship, *Grandcamp*, was in port to load American ammonium nitrate. This was produced during wartime for explosives but later recyled as fertilizer to send to Europe in Liberty ships to help farmers and the post-war recovery. On the morning of 16 April, as dockworkers completed loading some 2,300 tons of ammonium nitrate into the *Grandcamp*, someone saw smoke coming from the cargo holds. The fire quickly spread despite efforts to put it out. Not long after 9 am, barely an hour after the smoke was first spotted, the ship disintegrated in a massive explosion that was heard as far as 150 miles away.

A huge mushroom-shaped cloud billowed more than 2,000 feet into the sky. The rising shockwave knocked two light planes that were flying overhead out of the sky. Steel shards scythed through workers along the docks and a crowd of curious onlookers who had gathered at the head of the pier where the *Grandcamp* was moored. Many were killed instantly: the ship's crew, bystanders and almost the entire volunteer firefighter corps of the town. At the nearby Monsanto Chemical Company plant, 145 of the 450 shift workers on duty died. A 15-foot tidal wave thrown up by the explosion swept a large steel barge several hundred feet inland, carrying dead and injured people back into the blast zone as the water receded. Ignacio Hernandez, then a five-year-old living in Texas City, ran with his mother away from the blast. He remembers one woman wailing: "The world is coming to an end!"

Pieces of the *Grandcamp*, some weighing several tons, fell on the port and town for several minutes, extending the range of casualties and property damage well into the business district, about a mile away. The ship's anchor, weighing about 1.5 tons, was found two miles away, embedded 10 feet into the ground. Falling shrapnel bombarded buildings and oil storage tanks in refineries close to the port, releasing flammable liquids and starting numerous fires. In addition to ammonium nitrate, the *Grandcamp*'s cargo included large balls of sisal twine, bales of cotton, tobacco, peanuts, drilling equipment and a few cases of small arms ammunition. After the rain of shrapnel, came flaming balls of sisal and cotton, adding to the growing conflagration.

The horror did not end quickly. In darkness very early the following day, 17 April, another Liberty ship in the port, the *High Flyer*, carrying sulphur and about 1,000 tons of ammonium nitrate, also exploded. It had been severely damaged by the blast from the *Grandcamp*. Although casualties were light because rescue personnel had evacuated the dock area, the blast compounded already severe property damage. In what witnesses described as a giant fireworks display, incandescent chunks of steel from the ship arched high into the night sky, falling over a wide radius and starting many fires. Crude oil tanks burst into flames, and a chain reaction of explosions and heat spread fires to other structures that were still standing after the *Grandcamp* detonated. When dawn came, large columns of thick, black smoke were visible 30 miles away. These clouds hovered over Texas City for days until the fires gradually burned themselves out or were extinguished by weary fire-fighting crews.

Power and water were cut off. Almost 4,000 rescue workers and volunteers from surrounding cities responded with assistance. Temporary hospitals, morgues and shelters were set up. Eventually, the Red Cross and the Texas Department of Public Safety released a death toll of 568. It included 405 dead who could be identified and another 63 who could not. An additional 100 persons were classified as "believed missing" because no trace of their remains could be found. An estimated 3,500 people were injured — about 25 per cent of the town's 16,000 population. The port and its industrial zone were devastated. Property damage amounted to well over US$1 billion in today's dollars. One third of Texas City's just over 1,500 houses were condemned, leaving 2,000 people homeless and exacerbating an already-serious post war housing shortage. Investigators came to the conclusion that a discarded cigarette triggered the *Grandcamp* blast.[42]

Imagine what might happen if a ship, like the *Baltic Sky*, loaded with hundreds of tons of ammonium nitrate was hijacked by terrorists and exploded in a major port-city in Asia, North America or Europe close to oil or chemical storage areas, refineries, petrochemical processing complexes or other industries that use inflammable or toxic materials? Or imagine if the ship was blown up near densely populated zones?

4 Mega-Terror — Radiological and Nuclear

The most dangerous possibility in maritime terrorism — indeed it is a nightmare scenario for many Western and Asian officials and analysts — is that terrorists might sooner or later:

- get and use a powerful radiological bomb, in which conventional explosives disperse deadly radioactive poison; or
- even a nuclear bomb, perhaps concealed in the one of over 230 million containers that move through the world's ports each year.

How could this happen? What would be the consequences of such an attack and the extent to which it could disrupt world trade? And what is being done to prevent it? The rest of this book seeks to answer these questions.

Political Economy of Terror

Al-Qaeda understands the political economy of terror. It aims for an ever more costly impact on the US, its allies and friends in the Middle East and elsewhere, and countries that support the US and British-led coalition in Iraq. The US government says that Al-Qaeda's central focus on economic targets is consistent with its stated ideological goals and longstanding strategy, to undermine what the terrorists see as the backbone of US power — the economy and the critical transportation infrastructure at home and abroad that sustains it. Striking a prominent US target for economic and symbolic reasons would have immediate worldwide impact.[1]

Two audio tapes purportedly from Al-Qaeda's leader Osama bin Laden that were broadcast in October 2003 by Qatar-based Arabic television station Al Jazeera said that the group would launch more attacks inside and outside the United States and said that all countries backing the US occupation of Iraq were targets. The broadcast specifically named Britain, Spain, Australia, Poland, Japan, Italy and Muslim states, especially Kuwait and other Gulf states.[2]

US officials have warned repeatedly that shipping and trade are among Al-Qaeda's prime targets and that a terrorist attack on the maritime transportation system would have a devastating and long-lasting impact on global shipping, international trade and the world economy.[3]

Following its use of a small boat packed with explosives in October 2002 to set the giant French tanker *Limburg* ablaze off Yemen, Al-Qaeda claimed responsibility in these terms: "If a boat that didn't cost US$1,000 managed to devastate an oil tanker of that magnitude, so imagine the extent of the danger that threatens the West's commercial lifeline, which is petroleum. The operation of attacking the French tanker is not merely an attack against a tanker, it is an attack against international oil transport lines..." added the communique issued by Al-Qaeda's political bureau on 13 October, 2002.[4]

The Cost of 9/11

Banking and insurance losses from the attacks on the US in September 2001 have exceeded US$55 billion. Bin Laden has proclaimed that if his forces succeed in taking over Saudi Arabia, the global oil price will hit US$125 a barrel, a level that would cripple economies in the West and Asia. Bin Laden's deputy, Ayman Al Zawahiri, has stated that US economic targets are high on Al-Qaeda's hit list.[5]

Along with other risk factors, uncertainty resulting from perceptions that the international terrorist threat is increasing is turning the world into a more unstable place to do business, adding to commercial costs and deterring corporate expansion. This may well be part of the Al-Qaeda network's calculations. Aon Corporation's Trade Credit and Political Risk group, based in Chicago, reported in early 2004 that rising political risk could cost the world economy US$1 trillion this year in reduced corporate spending, investments and growth. The comparable figure for 2003 was more than US$800 billion.

According to Aon, the global cost of political risk has increased since the terrorist attacks on the US in September 2001. Before that date, political risk was estimated to cost the global economy US$200 billion annually. Of course, such risk includes legal and regulatory changes, environmental and human rights issues, changes in government and business policy, and currency crises as well as terrorism. But the latter is a major influence.[6]

Radiological Terrorism

A radiological, or so-called "dirty bomb" is a conventional explosive such as dynamite or ammonium nitrate that has been packaged with radioactive material, which scatters when the bomb goes off. It kills or injures through the initial blast of the conventional explosive and by spreading life-threatening radiation particles; hence the term "dirty". A dirty bomb contains radioactive material, but does not use that material to produce a nuclear explosion.

Such a bomb may not be a real weapon of mass destruction, when compared to a nuclear explosion that could cause hundreds of thousands of deaths and injuries in a big city. But a radiological bomb would certainly be a weapon of mass disruption and panic if detonated in or near a metropolis. Indeed, some US officials have said that dirty bombs, which could be constructed with relative ease by conventional bomb makers, may become the next weapons of choice for terrorists who want to cause panic and economic distruption.[7]

Depending on the sophistication and size of the radiological bomb, the radioactive material it dispersed, wind conditions, the location of the attack, and the speed with which the area was evacuated, the number of deaths and injuries from a dirty bomb might not be substantially greater than from a conventional bomb explosion. But panic over radioactivity and evacuation measures could snarl a city. Moreover, the area struck would be off-limits for at least several months during contamination clean-up efforts. This could paralyze a local economy and reinforce public fears about being near a radioactive zone.

The Federation of American Scientists (FAS) told a Senate panel in March 2002 that radioactive materials could easily be stolen from, or lost by, US research institutions and commercial sites and find their way into the hands of terrorists. Such materials could then be incorporated in a dirty bomb that might contaminate tens of city blocks, requiring prompt evacuation and creating terror in large communities, even if radiation casualties were low.

Areas as large as tens of square miles could be contaminated at levels that exceed recommended civilian exposure limits, the FAS said. Since there are often no effective ways to decontaminate buildings that have been exposed, demolition may be the only practical solution. If such an event were to take place in a city like New York, it would result in huge losses.

A radiological bomb attack could shut a port area for months for expensive decontamination. A severe attack could make large parts of a port-city uninhabitable for much longer.[8]

Theft and Trafficking

Radioactive materials are widely used and dispersed around the world, not just for military purposes or for fuelling nuclear reactors to generate electricity. Weapons-grade uranium and plutonium are under close guard. Highly radioactive spent fuel from nuclear reactors is also placed in safe and secure places.

But there are millions of other radioactive sources that have been distributed worldwide over the past 50 years, with hundreds of thousands currently being used, stored and produced. The radiation from radioactive isotopes provides a low-cost way to disinfect food, sterilize medical equipment, treat certain kinds of cancer, find oil deep underground, check the welding in pipelines, monitor water aquifers, build sensitive smoke detectors and provide other important economic services.

As a result, radioactive materials are used in many thousands of hospital and medical centres, research laboratories, oil drilling facilities, food irradiation plants and other sites. Some are under government control; others in the hands of universities and the private sector. Many are not properly secured or accounted for — they have been lost, stolen or abandoned.

IAEA Warning

The International Atomic Energy Agency (IAEA), has warned that the radioactive materials needed to build a dirty bomb can be found in almost any country in the world, and that more than 100 countries may have inadequate control and monitoring programmes to prevent or even detect the theft of these materials. It has located at least 20,000 operators of significant radioactive sources worldwide. They include over 10,000 radiotherapy units for medical care, 12,000 radiography units, and about 300 irradiator facilities for industrial applications.

The IAEA is the United Nations agency that sets world standards for nuclear safety and security, and acts as a watchdog against diversion or illicit use of nuclear materials. Although 134 countries are members of the IAEA and can benefit from its assistance, over 50 countries are not.

The IAEA says that while radioactive sources may number in the millions, only a small percentage have enough strength to cause serious harm because they contain potentially lethal amounts of radioactivity. They include cobalt-60, strontium-90, caesium-137 and iridium-192 used in industrial radiography, radiotherapy, industrial irradiators and thermo-electric generators. These isotopes emit intense gamma rays that are useful in killing bacteria and cancer cells. The rays can penetrate clothing and skin to enter the human body.

Fortunately, building the most potent radiological bombs using these isotopes is much more difficult for terrorists than assembling explosives to disperse less toxic material. Not only are the very dangerous substances more difficult to obtain, the successful spreading of highly radioactive particles could only be done by a terrorist organization that had access to specialized scientific knowledge.

The Federation of American Scientists says that alpha particle emitters such as plutonium and americium could also be used in a dirty bomb to create a long-term health hazard and should be closely controlled as well. The alpha particles cannot penetrate clothing or skin but if inhaled can cause cancer. Plutonium, which is used in nuclear weapons, also has non-military functions. In the 1960s and 1970s, the US government encouraged the use of plutonium in university facilities studying nuclear engineering and nuclear physics. Americium is used in smoke detectors and devices that find oil sources.

Since 1993, the IAEA has compiled a list of at least 263 confirmed cases of trafficking or unauthorized movement of radioactive materials but admits that the actual number of cases is likely to be significantly larger, not least because only about 70 states are collecting and sharing information on such trafficking with the IAEA. Of the cases brought to the IAEA's attention, the great majority appear to have involved opportunists or unsophisticated criminals, motivated by the hope of profit. But an important fraction of the cases involved persons who expected to find buyers interested in the radioactive contents of stolen sources and their ability to cause or threaten harm. Criminals are now trading in components and materials for dirty bombs. Indeed, authorities report a dangerous surge of interest from this quarter that is complicating an already difficult task confronting governments: how to stop terrorists from acquiring powerful radiological sources.

IAEA Director General, Mohamed ElBaradei, says that in the wake of the terrorist attacks on the US in September 2001 using civilian airliners to cause mass casualties and damage, "and the stark awareness of the potential for radioactive sources to be used in malevolent acts, source security has taken on a new urgency". He added: "What is needed is cradle-to-grave control of powerful radioactive sources to protect them against terrorism or theft".[9]

Missing Radioactive Material

The IAEA, the US Department of Energy and the Russian Federation's Ministry for Atomic Energy agreed in June 2002 to develop a coordinated and proactive strategy to locate, recover, secure and recyle the missing, or "orphaned", radioactive sources throughout the former Soviet Union. Many of the devices were abandoned after the Soviet breakup in 1991.

But a year after the recovery initiative was launched, the General Accounting Office (GAO), the investigative arm of the US Congress, said that thousands of containers of radioactive materials that can be used to build dirty bombs were still missing, particularly from the former Soviet Union. Meanwhile, the Los Alamos National Laboratory, an arm of the US Energy Department, concluded in a report in September 2003 that the security improvements under way "are unlikely to significantly alter the global risk picture for a few years".

The GAO warning came in June 2003 as authorities in Thailand, acting on a tip-off from US customs agents, arrested a Thai who was offering to sell a small quantity of radioactive cesium-137 to anyone prepared to pay US$240,000. He promised to show the buyer where as much as 30 kilograms of the cesium, that reportedly came from the former Soviet Union, was hidden in two separate stashes across the border in Laos .

The Thai affair is just one of many trafficking cases in recent years stretching from Russia and the former Soviet republics, to Europe, Asia, Africa and Latin America. These cases show that the radioactive materials needed to build dirty bombs could emerge nearly anywhere.[10]

Al-Qaeda and the Dirty Bomb

The British Broadcasting Corporation (BBC) reported in January 2003 that it had been presented with evidence by British officials which showed that Al-Qaeda had been trying to assemble radioactive material to build a radiological bomb and may have succeeded in assembling a small dirty bomb in a nuclear laboratory in the Afghan city of Herat. This was before US-led forces invaded Afghanistan in October 2001 to oust the Taliban regime that had allowed Al-Qaeda and Osama bin Laden to train terrorists and organize international terrorist operations from Afghanistan. The alleged dirty bomb was never recovered. But British officials said that Al-Qaeda certainly had the expertise to build another. They showed the BBC Al-Qaeda training manuals that set out details on how to use a dirty bomb to maximum effect.[11]

No dirty bomb attacks have ever been recorded. But the United Nations has reported that Iraq tested a one-ton radiological bomb in 1987. It said Iraq did not pursue the experiment because the radiation levels generated by the bomb were not deadly enough to make it effective against military targets.

However, many counter-terrorism officials and analysts fear that a dirty bomb attack by terrorists, to carry their fight to a new threshold of horror, panic and disruption, is inevitable. Eliza Manningham-Buller, the Director-General of MI5, Britain's domestic security service, said in June 2003 that it was only a matter of time before a terrorist attack using chemical, biological, radiological or nuclear technology was launched by Al-Qaeda or its affiliates against a big city in the West. "My conclusion, based on the intelligence we have uncovered, is that we are faced with the realistic possibility of some form of unconventional attack", she said.

The widespread availability of radiological bomb sources prompted scientists at the Los Alamos National Laboratory in the US to conclude, in its study released in September 2003, that a dirty bomb "attack somewhere in the world is overdue".

"Radiological terrorism is a very plausible threat", said Steven Koonin, a physicist and national security expert, who is provost of the California Institute of Technology. The CIA says that Al-Qaeda is interested in radiological bombs and that constructing one is "well within its capabilities as radiological materials are relatively easy to acquire from industrial or medical sources".[12]

A well-executed dirty bomb attack on a US city could expose hundreds of people to potentially lethal amounts of radiation, cause great panic and enormous economic losses, a 12-month study funded by the Pentagon and published in January 2004 concluded. "The threat of a radiological attack on the United States is real, and terrorists have a broad palette of (radioactive) isotopes to choose from", said the report by the Center for Technology and National Security Policy at the National Defence University. "It could cause tens of hundreds of fatalities under the right circumstances, and is essentially certain to cause great panic and enormous economic losses".[13]

The US Dirty Bomber

In June 2002, the US government announced that it had arrested Jose Padilla, an American citizen and suspected Al-Qaeda operative, on his return to the US, thus disrupting "an unfolding terrorist plot to attack the United States by exploding a radioactive 'dirty bomb'". Padilla, a former Chicago gang member with a long criminal record, had been in detention since May 2002 when he was taken into custody at Chicago's O'Hare International Airport after arriving on a flight from Pakistan. He was carrying over US$10,000 in cash.

US Attorney General John Ashcroft said that Padilla, who had converted to Islam and was sometimes known as Abdullah al Mujajir and Ibrahim Padilla, trained with Al-Qaeda, including studying how to wire explosive devices and researching radiological dispersion devices. Ashcroft said that Al-Qaeda knew that as a US citizen, Padilla would be able to travel freely in America without drawing attention to himself. He added that Padilla, aged about 32, was exploring a plan to build and explode a radioactive bomb.[14]

In August 2002, US prosecutors revealed further details in the case against Padilla in documents presented to a New York court. It said that after his release from prison in the US in the early 1990s, Padilla travelled to Pakistan, Egypt, Saudi Arabia and Afghanistan, and became closely associated with the Al-Qaeda network, meeting with senior leaders of the group on several occasions while in Afghanistan and Pakistan in 2001 and 2002. The government told the court that Padilla discussed with senior Al-Qaeda operatives terrorist attacks in the US, including the plan to detonate a dirty bomb.

An unclassified memo by a special adviser to the US Defense Department on terrorist suspects filed separately with the New York court said that Padilla conducted research on a "uranium-enhanced" explosive device at an Al-Qaeda safehouse in Lahore, Pakistan, and that he planned to use radioactive material stolen in the US to build it. Prosecutors said that information about Padilla's activities came from several confidential sources, including two Al-Qaeda associates being detained outside the US.

US officials said that Padilla had proposed the plan to build and detonate a radiological device, possibly in the US capital, Washington, to Abu Zubaydah, then Al-Qaeda's top terrorism coordinator and a senior lieutenant of Osama bin Laden. Zubaydah was arrested in Pakistan in March 2002 and handed over to the US for interrogation. US officials said that Padilla first met Zubaydah in Afghanistan in 2001and that they later travelled together to several locations in Pakistan.[15]

In June 2002, US President George Bush designated Padilla as an "enemy combatant", which meant the military could hold him indefinitely without bringing him to trial or giving him access to a lawyer. Bush had signed an order transferring Padilla to the custody of the US Defense Department, saying that he represented a "continuing, present and grave danger" to national security. The president's authority was challenged by Padilla's lawyers and in December 2003 the US Second Circuit Court of Appeals, in a 2 to 1 ruling, said it was illegal for the government to hold him in military custody and said he should be released within 30 days. The court said that the government could transfer Padilla to a civilian authority. The US government described the court's decision as flawed and said it would seek to halt the ruling pending further judicial review.[16]

The US Supreme Court announced on 20 February 2004 that it would rule on this crucial — and fiercely debated — element of President Bush's legal strategy in the war against terrorism: his assertion of authority to declare US citizens captured on American soil "enemy combatants" and detain them indefinitely without charges or access to counsel. The justices outlined an expedited briefing schedule that would enable them to hear the case by the last week of April 2004 and decide it by July. In March 2004, Padilla was permitted to meet with his attorney for the first time. But the Pentagon said that the lawyer's meeting with Padilla was discretionary and would be "subject to appropriate security restrictions".[17]

How far advanced was the plot to build and explode a dirty bomb in the US, how well qualified was Padilla to build it, and did he have associates or co-conspirators in America?

US officials admit the plan had not progressed far. FBI Director Robert Mueller said it was "in the discussion stage. And it had not gone, as far as we know, much past the discussion stage, but there were substantial discussions undertaken". US officials would not comment on whether Padilla had co-conspirators in America.

But some analysts were sceptical about Padilla's technical qualifications as an explosives expert, saying that he had brought Al-Qaeda "laughably inaccurate" instructions to make a hydrogen bomb that were taken from the Internet. Padilla was urged by terrorist commanders to focus on a conventional explosive combined with radioactive material. These analysts said that his arrest indicated that Al-Qaeda was turning to "irregulars" such as Padilla and Richard Reid — a British citizen accused of trying to blow up an American Airlines flight from Paris to Miami in December 2001 using one of his shoes as a bomb — to carry out attacks instead of highly trained and disciplined agents like those responsible for the devastation in New York and Washington in September 2001.[18]

The British Dirty Bomber

Still, concerns about the risk of terrorists getting and using dirty bombs intensified in December 2003 when US prosecutors said that a British arms dealer, held in the US on charges of trying to sell shoulder-fired missiles to shoot down airliners, would face additional charges of plotting to procure a dirty bomb. <u>Hemant Lakhani, 68, who was born in India but holds a British passport</u>, was arrested in August 2003 in an sting operation involving intelligence agencies from the US, Britain and Russia. He was detained at a hotel near Newark International Airport and charged with trying to sell a missile imported from Russia to an FBI informant.[19]

Nuclear Terrorism

Graham Allison, a former US assistant secretary of defence who now directs the Belfer Centre for Science and International Affairs at Harvard's Kennedy School of Government, is on record as saying that he believes "the single largest, most urgent threat to Americans today is nuclear terrorism. The ship, I think, is one of the most dangerous delivery devices. A weapon or (fissile) material in the belly of a ship has been one of the nightmare scenarios for people who think about how nuclear weapons might arrive in the US".

He says that he worries about the devastation and disruption that would be caused by a nuclear terrorist attack on a major port-city. Even if a small nuclear bomb exploded in New York or Boston, it would kill half a million people, he adds.[20]

"No weapon is beyond the planning of terrorist groups, particularly the Al-Qaeda network", the US Energy Secretary Spencer Abraham said in August 2003 when he announced an agreement with the Dutch government to install sophisticated detection equipment to find nuclear and other radioactive material hidden in containers at Europe's largest seaport in Rotterdam, the Netherlands. "Terrorist groups and rogue nations trying to smuggle components for nuclear weapons is a serious threat that must be addressed", he added. Rotterdam, which handles more than 300 million metric tons of cargo each year, is one of the first sites outside the US to use the new detection equipment. It was developed by US Department of Energy laboratories as part of America's nuclear security programme to guard against proliferation of weapons materials.[21]

There is no evidence that Al-Qaeda or any other terrorist group has nuclear weapons. But they have shown interest in acquiring them. In the mid-1990s, Al-Qaeda agents tried repeatedly — though without success — to purchase bomb-grade highly enriched uranium in Africa, Europe and Russia. In November 2001, Osama bin Laden announced that he had obtained a nuclear weapon, but US intelligence officials dismissed his claims. Documents recovered from Afghanistan after the fall of the Taliban regime also described Al-Qaeda's nuclear ambitions. One of the documents recovered from an Al-Qaeda facility in Afghanistan contained a sketch of a crude nuclear device. Two retired Pakistani nuclear scientists were detained in late 2001 after meeting Osama bin Laden in Afghanistan. They were later released by the Pakistan government without being charged, despite suspicions that the purpose of the meeting was to discuss how Al-Qaeda could make or acquire nuclear bombs. The CIA believes that Al-Qaeda was seeking a nuclear explosive device — and still is.[22]

Nuclear weapons are in the hands of only eight countries (nine, if North Korea has at least two crude bombs, as the CIA suspects). These arsenals are supposed to be closely guarded, although concerns have been expressed about the security of some military facilities, notably in Pakistan and the former Soviet Union which broke up to become Russia and 14 other countries. By some estimates, half of the former Soviet arsenal is inadequately protected, although Russian authorities deny this.

While less than ten states are known to have nuclear weapons, an additional two dozen countries have research reactors with enough highly enriched uranium (HEU) to build at least one nuclear bomb on their own. Nuclear weapons normally have an explosive core containing over 90 per cent of uranium-235. It is estimated that the global nuclear inventory includes more than 30,000 nuclear weapons, and enough HEU and plutonium for 240,000 more. Theft or diversion of bomb-grade material from military nuclear facilities is a risk. But theft or diversion from civilian nuclear facilities, or a physical attack or act of sabotage designed to cause an uncontrolled release of radioactivity into the surrounding environment, are considered a bigger risk.

There are some 440 nuclear power reactors operating around the world to generate electricity. There are approximately 650 nuclear research reactors designed to produce radiation sources used in medicine, industry, agriculture and for research. Less than 290 of these relatively small reactors are working. There are also 250 nuclear fuel cycle plants, including uranium mills and facilities that convert, enrich, store and reprocess nuclear material.[23]

Building a Nuke

Could terrorists build a nuclear bomb? Experts say it would not be easy. Several very difficult problems would have to be solved simultaneously. Acquiring the fissionable material to generate a nuclear explosion is the single most difficult step. At least 25 kilograms (55 pounds) of highly enriched uranium would be needed to make a crude bomb, or roughly 8 kilograms (17.6 pounds) of plutonium, a much more difficult and dangerous material to work with.

Other problems would include recruiting scientific experts in a broad range of disciplines, obtaining specialized industrial equipment and avoiding the chemical and radiological hazards inherent in working with nuclear materials and high explosives. This would probably take many years. Iraq, for instance, tried throughout the 1980s and 1990s to build a nuclear bomb but failed — despite ample funding, readily available infrastructure and equipment, and a dedicated research team. The task would be even harder for a terrorist group without the resources of a state.

But experts note that building a crude, bulky, low-yield nuclear weapon — which the CIA calls an Improvised Nuclear Device (IND) — would be far easier than making the compact, reliable, high-yield weapons found in US arsenals. An IND could be smuggled to its target by ship, container or truck. The potential consequences of terrorists acquiring a nuclear explosive device would be so devastating and disruptive that it must be a matter of serious concern, even if the chances of it happening appear slim.[24]

A study by the US Institute for Science and International Security in 2002 concluded that Al-Qaeda would be capable of building a crude nuclear bomb — one that could be delivered by ship or truck — if it had the right amount of enriched uranium, about 45 kilograms, or 100 pounds. Other experts say that 60 kilograms would be needed to make a first-generation bomb similar to the one that the US used in 1945 to destroy the Japanese city of Hiroshima and help bring about the surrender of Japan and the end of World War II.[25]

Slow-Moving Global Partnership

To secure fissionable materials for making nuclear bombs and prevent them from reaching terrorists, the Group of Eight nations — the US, Britain, Japan, France, Germany, Italy, Russia and Canada — launched the Global Partnership Against the Spread of Weapons of Mass Destruction at their summit meeting in Kananaskis, Canada, in June 2002. They pledged to raise up to US$20 billion over the next 10 years to reduce the risk that unsecured weapons or materials of mass destruction might fall into the hands of terrorists. Since the Global Partnership was announced, the EU, Norway, Sweden, Finland and the Netherlands have joined. The 14 members have initiated or extended dozens of projects, totalling over US$1 billion in 2003 alone, for work on dismantling nuclear submarines, destroying chemical weapons, securing nuclear materials and reemploying nuclear technicians, mainly in the former Soviet Union. But critics says much more needs to be done, particularly in securing weapons and bomb-grade material.

In October 2003 a report funded by the US-based Nuclear Threat Initiative, an anti-proliferation watchdog co-chaired by former US Senator and arms control expert Sam Nunn, highlighted the danger of more than 130 civilian research reactors in 40 countries around the world. They use highly enriched uranium fuel and many of the reactors have "no more security than a night watchman and a chain-link fence". Most of the HEU fuel would need some chemical processing before it could be used in a bomb. But this processing is straightforward and the relevant chemistry openly published. Moreover, the spent fuel elements from research reactors are typically small, easy to carry away and have radioactively levels too low to deter suicidal terrorists. This is in contrast to spent fuel from nuclear power reactors which is massive and so intensely radioactive that potential thieves would likely be incapacitated by radiation effects as they tried to steal it.

Highly enriched uranium is the easiest material from which to make a nuclear bomb and might well be within within the capabilities of the Al-Qaeda network. Making a "gun-type" bomb — the type that obliterated Hiroshima — from HEU involves little more than slamming two pieces of HEU together fast enough. The Hiroshima bomb was a cannon-fired barrel that propelled a shell of HEU into rings of HEU. Making a bomb from plutonium would require an "implosion-type" design, in which explosive lenses arranged around a plutonium ball crush it to a smaller size. This would be much more difficult for terrorists to accomplish — but still cannot be entirely ruled out.[26]

The uranium used in nuclear power plants to generate electricity is useless for nuclear bomb building. But the plutonium used in — and produced by — civilian power plants could theoretically be used in a nuclear weapon, although separating such "reactor grade" plutonium is a difficult and hazardous process. Though the threat that terrorists could use this route to make a bomb is considered small, nuclear specialists say it is imperative to monitor and protect sources of plutonium as well as HEU.[27]

Officials who track weapons of mass destruction-related trafficking say they cannot rule out the possibility of terrorists acquiring enough fissile material to build a primitive nuclear weapon, given the vulnerability of such material to theft and the increasing professionalism of nuclear smuggling. According to the IAEA, since 1993 there have been around 400 instances of trafficking in nuclear fuel or other radioactive materials. In all, about 26 pounds of enriched uranium and almost a pound of plutonium have been seized in various arrests — far less than terrorists would need to make a single bomb. But the reported instances may not reflect the actual scale of trafficking.[28]

Open Sesame

The recent exposure of an extensive and long-running nuclear black market based in Pakistan that peddled weapons technology to Libya, Iran, North Korea, and perhaps other places, has amplified fears about the spread of nuclear weapons and the prospect of terrorists acquiring them. The revelations starting early in 2004 about this clandestine international trafficking in technology and equipment to build nuclear weapons showed how widely available dangerous material and knowledge had become. The sales had begun at least as far back as the late 1980s.

In his televised confession on 4 February 2004, Pakistani scientist Abdul Qadir Khan said that he had sold nuclear secrets to foreign countries. According to Pakistani, US and IAEA officials, those countries included Libya, Iran and North Korea. They received equipment that was either exported from Pakistan or procured in Europe, Asia and South Africa by Khan and his network of associates. They had developed a sophisticated supply chain that offered technical advice, parts, shipping and customer support, prompting the head of IAEA, Mohamed ElBaradei, to call it the "Wal-Mart of private-sector proliferation". Yet many analysts say the Khan network could not have operated without the knowledge and approval at very senior levels of Pakistan's armed forces and intelligence service.

The equipment included centrifuges for enriching uranium so that it can be used in nuclear warheads. In the case of Libya, which agreed in December 2003 to get rid of its weapons of mass destruction under international inspection, the Pakistan-based supply network provided not just centrifuge systems for making highly enriched uranium but also nuclear warhead designs of an old (1960s vintage) but reliable type that appear to have orginated from China in the early 1980s. One of the things investigators urgently want to discover is whether North Korea, Iran and perhaps other countries and terrorist groups received nuclear bomb making instructions and materials via the Khan black market.[29]

Hiroshima and Nagasaki

The two nuclear bombs dropped by the US on Hiroshima and Nagasaki in Japan in August 1945 to hasten the end of World War II destroyed both cities, turning them into mass graveyards poisoned by radioactive contamination.

The fissile core of the Hiroshima bomb was made of highly enriched uranium 235. It released a fireball of energy equivalent to 12.5 kilotons, or 12,500 tons of TNT, causing severe burns and loss of eyesight. Thermal burns of bare skin occurred as far as 3.5 kilometres from ground zero, directly below the explosion point about 580 metres above central Hiroshima. Most people exposed to thermal rays within a one-kilometre radius of ground zero died. Tiles and glass melted in the intense heat. All combustible materials were consumed.

An atomic explosion causes an enormous shock wave followed instantaneously by a rapid expansion of air in an immensely powerful blast with typhonic winds. Concrete buildings near ground zero, hit by the blast from above, had ceilings crushed and windows and doors blown out. Many people were trapped under fallen structures and burned to death. Being anywhere within 500 metres of ground zero was fatal. People exposed at distances of 3 to 5 kilometres later showed symptoms of after-effects, including cancers induced by radiation.

The death count in Hiroshima in the wake of the atomic bombing is estimated to have reached 140,000 by the end of December, 1945. In Nagasaki, which was razed by a plutonium bomb, around 70,000 people were thought to have died by the end of 1945.

A crude nuclear bomb with the explosive power of 10,000 tons of TNT (smaller than the Hiroshima bomb), if detonated in mid-town Manhattan on a typical workday, could kill half a million people and cause over US$1 trillion in direct economic damage.[30]

Chernobyl

Many of those who died in Hiroshima and Nagasaki did so from the effects of radiation. This, too, was the major killer in the world's biggest peacetime nuclear disaster. It happened when the Chernobyl nuclear power reactor that generated electricity in Ukraine exploded in April 1986, contaminating vast areas of Belarus, Ukraine and Russia. The United Nations estimated that early in 2004, nearly 18 years after the accident occurred, more than seven million people still suffered from the effects. Radiation poisoning has caused a large increase in thyroid cancer among children, other forms of cancer in the general population as well as long-term genetic disorders. Many people also suffer from psychological problems.

The UN found that 23 per cent of Belarus, the hardest hit area, was still contaminated by radiation and would remain so for hundreds of years to come. Huge tracts of forests and once-fertile agricultural land have been abandoned, raising the possibility that a big forest fire or flood could spread the radioactivity more widely in Europe.[31]

5 Catastrophic Terrorism and its Potential Impact on Global Trade

A nuclear 9/11 would make the World Trade Center attacks look like a warning shot. It would be impossible to calculate the economic costs, because there is no way to calculate how long it would take for citizens to recover the confidence they need to spend and invest. The public would assume that if the terrorists had one nuclear weapon, they could get another. If they would use it in one city, they would use it in another. If even one goes off, it's hard to see how we could recover. We have to prevent if from happening — ever.

Former US Senator and arms control expert, Sam Nunn, who co-chairs the Nuclear Threat Initiative.

The use of either a nuclear or powerful radiological bomb in a major port-city would cut the arteries of maritime commerce if it was believed to have come by sea. It would halt much of the world's trade and severely damage the global economy, as governments scrambled to put in place extra security measures to protect their people, cities and economies. Such measures would be drastic and include: lengthy cargo inspections in the ports of the affected country, as well as in ports of nations that did extensive sea trade with it, or even the complete closure of ports for an indefinite period, while extra checks and safeguards were put in place to allay public anxiety.

One of the first things the US government did after the terrorist attacks in September 2001, was to shut US airspace and ground all civilian flights for four days — a security measure to protect the American public that had severe repercussions on aviation, travel, tourism and business around the world, including in Asia, as hundreds of scheduled flights had to be cancelled or diverted. The Bush administration also closed US ports for two days.[1]

Costs of a Terrorist Attack

How much would a major terrorist attack on shipping or maritime infrastructure cost and what impact would it have on just-in-time delivery for companies? Since such an attack has not happened, no one knows the precise answers to these questions. They would, of course, depend on the severity of the attack, the extent of casualties and damage, and the nature of public and government reaction to them.

US West Coast Port Lockout

In a bitter dispute between unions and management, all 29 American ports on the west coast of the US closed for nearly a fortnight in October 2002. These ports handle approximately 42 per cent of US maritime imports and exports by value. The shutdown delayed more than 200 ships carrying 300,000 containers. As a result, railcars and inter-modal shipments were parked across the US as American and Asian exports filled warehouses, freezers and grain elevators. Ships made costly diversions to other ports and many businesses laid off workers or cut production.

The lockout and the weeks of efforts to clear the cargo backlog imposed substantial costs on American exporters and importers. One estimate of the direct costs of delivery delay alone was US$467 million. But the port closure had been foreseen. So companies were able to take steps well in advance to build stocks to mitigate its impact. This is something they could not do in a port-related terrorist attack that came without warning.

During the shutdown, importers with time-sensitive and perishable cargo faced the greatest losses. Many other importers said that if the closure was prolonged, they were ready to consider radical supply-chain changes to meet their production and retail needs. These included paying for more expensive air freight and/or longer ocean shipping through the Panama Canal and ports on the east coast of the US, to changing their supplier base to non-Asian sources.

The disruption and clearance of the backlog lasted for about a month. It cost Asian economies an average of 0.4 per cent of nominal GDP. The negative impact in Hong Kong, Singapore and Malaysia was estimated to be as high as 1.1 per cent of nominal GDP.[2]

Just-in-time to Just-in-case

Fear of a terrorist strike that would disrupt transport systems may already have added tens of billions of dollars in costs to the US economy since September 2001. One Michigan State University study indicates that manufacturers in the US increased their inventory holdings in 2002 as a precaution against further terrorist trouble. In 2001, average large American companies held 1.36 months of stocks, down from 1.57 months in the early 1990s. The 2001 figure was projected to rise to 1.43 months in 2002 as firms held more "just-in-case" inventory. According to the study, the threat of terrorist attacks had erased about half the logistics productivity gains realized in the US in the previous decade, and could have added between US$50 billion and US$80 billion to business costs in the US alone in 2002.[3]

Economic and Trade Impacts of 9/11

The terrorist attacks on the US in 2001 resulted directly in the destruction of physical assets estimated at US$14 billion for private businesses, US$1.5 billion for state and local governments, and US$0.7 billion for the federal government. Cleanup and rescue costs have been estimated at US$11 billion. The attacks occurred when business growth in the US was slowing and they further dented waning confidence. Economic growth forecasts were quickly revised downwards by an additional 0.5 percentage points. Specific sectors like airlines, tourism and hotels were hit particularly hard. The insurance sector faced an unprecedented catastrophe, with losses estimated between US$30–60 billion.

In response to the crisis, the US Federal Reserve injected massive amounts of liquidity into the economy. Interest rates tumbled to as low as 1.2 per cent on 19 September, 2001, eight days after the terrorists struck. Central Banks around the world followed suit in taking action to lower interest rates substantially. The fiscal response was rapid too. In the US, an emergency spending package of some US$40 billion was approved. An additional US$5 billion in direct grants and US$10 billion in loans were given to US airlines to help them stay in business until travel picked up again. Stricter limits applied in Europe, where Belgium's Sabena airline and Swissair went bankrupt.

The costs of trading, at least in the short-term, have increased because of the additional security requirements and additional risks associated with trade. But there is great uncertainty, both on the size of these extra costs and on their likely long-term repercussions on trade. Administrative costs of trade, including customs, are estimated to amount to between 2 per cent and 7 per cent of the value of trade. Transport costs vary from about 1 per cent of the value for goods like pharmaceuticals, to over 20 per cent for fertilizers. The risk is that higher transport and trading costs will reduce exports and imports. Some econometric studies estimate that each 1 per cent increase in such costs can cut trade by between 2 per cent and 3 per cent. While this may be an over-estimate, it does illustrate the potential risk of a major terrorist attack on the transport system.[4]

Port Security War Game

In October 2002, the US-based Conference Board of senior business executives and economists teamed up with the consulting firm Booz Allen and Hamilton. They assembled 85 high-level government and industry representatives to test their responses to a major crisis involving terrorist attacks using cargo containers shipped through North American ports. The war game scenario was based on a coordinated terrorist plot to smuggle in and detonate both radiological and conventional bombs.

The discovery of the first dirty bomb in the Port of Savannah created public panic that was magnified three days later by the detection of a second such bomb in a container transported from Thailand to the Port of Halifax in Canada and from there by truck to Minneapolis in the US. In response, US authorities closed all ports and border crossings indefinitely and stocks on Wall Street plunged. Petrol prices rose sharply because ships were unable to deliver fuel to a US economy that is heavily reliant on imported energy.

The simulation showed that even with round-the-clock inspections assisted by the US National Guard, only 20 per cent of incoming containers could be physically checked. So the need to reopen ports to prevent even more serious economic disruption quickly became evident. On day 10, Canada reopened its ports to ships unable to reach US ports as measures were agreed between the two countries to fast-track container inspections on the US-Canada border. Two days later, all US ports reopened for round-the-clock operations.

However on day 20, a railcar carrying a container of wine imported from France exploded in downtown Chicago. The container, which had a conventional bomb hidden among the wine crates, entered the US through the New York-New Jersey port complex. Share prices on Wall Street again plummeted, forcing a halt to trading. Port activity in the US gradually returned to normal over the next few weeks and by day 52, all cargo backlogs were reported to have been cleared. The container supply chain backlog took several weeks more to stabilize.

By the end of the simulated crisis on day 92, total estimated losses to the US economy amounted to 58 billion US dollars.[5]

Insurance

The potential direct cost of a terrorist attack on shipping or maritime infrastructure varies greatly according to the scope of the attack, its target and its location.

A single attack on a tanker, as happened in the case of the *Limburg*, had relatively low direct costs, mainly the oil that was lost when it spilled into the sea and had to be cleaned up, and repairing the damage to the ship. The *Limburg* stayed afloat after the oil fire was put out. Had terrorists attacked and sunk the tanker, spilling its oil or setting it ablaze in the nearby Bab el-Mandab Strait or the more distant Strait of Hormuz, the direct cost in disruption of shipping and trade could have been much higher.

This would also apply if a ship carrying ammonium nitrate or other explosive or inflammable material was blown up in a major port-city. As shown in the case of the Texas City disaster in 1947, there would be extensive loss of life, injury and damage to property.[6]

However, the direct harm of such an attack is likely to be dwarfed by indirect costs linked to reactions to the attack, especially insurance. The heavy insurance payouts for damage to property, loss of life and injury following September 2001 has profoundly changed the business and legal environment in which ocean marine insurers and underwriters operate. They have become much more sensitive to terrorist risk at sea, in ports or indeed anywhere along the worldwide cargo container supply chain. Insurance premiums for ships, their cargo, crew and marine liability have risen across the board, while exclusions from insurance coverage have been tightened.

Insurance against terrorism is vital for seaborne trade and the global economy. It is still available but it now costs substantially more than before September 2001. For example, marine insurance companies offer protection and indemnity (P&I) policies covering a ship's cargo and crew. They operate in P&I clubs to manage risks. After the attacks on the US, the clubs specifically identified terrorism as an exemption in their policies. It is placed under war risk in the Strikes, Riots and Civil Commotion (SRCC) category of marine insurance and requires additional premium coverage. In the US after

9/11, that rate went up on average by well over 50 per cent but evidently remains affordable. Importers and exporters usually buy cargo insurance policies, while ship owners or charterers more often purchase hull and liability insurance.

NBC, or nuclear, biological and chemical risks related to terrorism, are specifically excluded from coverage by the American Institute of Marine Underwriters and other insurers.[7]

Aden

What would happen to insurance rates if terrorists attacked, or worse still blocked, a major port, strait or waterway used for international trade?

The bigger the attack up the scale of terrorism, the greater the insurance shock would be. As noted above, there is no insurance for a maritime-related terrorist attack involving a nuclear bomb. The recovery costs would be unimaginably huge.

They would also be very heavy if a powerful radiological bomb was detonated in a mega port-city. Whether private insurance payouts would be available to aid recovery from a dirty bomb attack using conventional explosives to disperse radioactive toxins is doubtful.

Even a terrorist attack using a ship or ships to block a busy port, strait or waterway — but not involving nuclear or radiological bombs — would trigger a damaging upward spiral in insurance rates and make many ships avoid the area.

The fate of the port of Aden in the wake of the terrorist attack on the *Limburg* in October 2002 is an example. International shipping business collapsed, brought down by security fears and a hike in insurance premiums to prohibitively high levels. Marine underwriters in the influential Lloyd's of London market tripled war risk premiums for ships calling at Aden and other ports in Yemen to as high as 0.5 per cent of the value of the vessel's hull and machinery, compared to about 0.15 per cent before the attack — an increase amounting to hundreds of thousands of US dollars for larger ships. For a ship carrying around 5,600 standard twenty-foot containers (TEUs), this premium came to as much as US$300,000 per port call.

As a result, many vessels diverted to Salalah port in neighbouring Oman or stayed away from the area altogether. Container cargo arriving at the port, mainly from elsewere in the region for transshipment to a hub port overseas, plunged from 43,000 TEUs in September 2002, the month before the attack on the *Limburg*, to

3,000 TEUs just two months later. They then fell further, to almost nothing. In the third quarter of 2003, the Yemeni government claimed it had successfully negotiated a substantial reduction in the prohibitive war risk premiums.

But the damage to the shipping business had already been done. The previously booming two-berth Aden Container Terminal, 60 per cent owned by Singapore's PSA Corporation, was crippled by the business slump. PSA was forced to virtually write off its stake in 2002, in the form of a SG$125 million provision for impairment loss. In October 2003, Yemen's official news agency, Saba, reported that PSA had signed an agreement to end its port concession and hand the assets back to the Yemeni government, its 40 per cent partner in the project.[8]

The Bali Bombing and Indonesia as a War-risk Zone

The terrorist bombings in Bali in October 2002 showed how sensitive to terrorism marine insurers have become, even though the attacks were not maritime-related. Seaports across the entire Indonesian archipelago were declared unsafe by Lloyd's marine underwriters' association and added to a list of "exclusion" zones that also included at the time Somalia, the Congo, Libya and the Persian Gulf. The addition of Indonesia meant that a ship's existing insurance was cancelled if calling at any Indonesian port.[9]

Conclusions

Three broad conclusions emerge from the US west coast port shutdown, the Conference Board/Booz Allen Hamilton simulation exercise, and the experience of Yemen after the terrorist attack on the *Limburg* in October 2002:

- costs linked to terror-related trade disruptions rise exponentially over time, up to a certain threshold where supply chains undergo radical changes;
- major terrorist attacks using ships or cargo containers are likely to have the biggest impact on global trade because they are part of an inter-connected supply chain that stretches deep into the heart of many leading national economies; and
- the total costs of any such attacks are likely to be measured in tens of billions of dollars.

There are two important things to note, however. First, measures are being put in place by many leading international trading nations to prevent a serious maritime-related terrorist attack from happening. A lot of these security safeguards have already been applied and others are taking effect in 2004. Second, the potential damage from a major terrorist attack using ships or cargo containers is many times higher than the known and projected costs of the new maritime security requirements.[10]

6 Costs and Benefits of Enhanced Security

The new security measures for maritime trade are both multilateral and bilateral. A new international regime for port and ship security mandated by the IMO will take effect from July, 2004. Checks on seafarers are also being tightened. The ILO adopted a convention in June 2003 that provides for new seafarer identification documents with a biometric imprint.

In addition, various measures are being implemented by a wide range of countries outside the framework of the United Nations. Many are driven by initiatives put in place by the US to guard against terrorist strikes. Concerned at America's vulnerability to a catastrophic terrorist attack from the sea, the US government has turned its attention to securing seaborne trade and the interlocking global supply chain. The aim of all these anti-terrorist measures is to "retrofit" the global system of commerce to make it more secure while not unnecessarily impeding the flow of goods.[1]

IMO Regime

In the wake of the terrorist attacks on the US in September 2001, the IMO reviewed the state of maritime security. The IMO Conference of Contracting Governments to the International Convention for the Safety of Life at Sea, held from 9 to 13 December 2002, adopted a number of amendments to the 1974 Safety of Life at Sea Convention (SOLAS). The most far-reaching are encompassed in the new International Ship and Port Facility Code (ISPS).

The Code contains detailed security-related requirements for governments, port authorities and shipping companies in a mandatory section (Part A), together with a series of guidelines on how to meet these requirements in a second, non-mandatory section (Part B). The IMO Conference in December 2002 also adopted a series of resolutions designed to add weight to the amendments, encourage the application of the measures to ships and port facilities not covered by the Code and pave the way for future work on the subject.

The mandatory measures include:

- installation of satellite-based automatic tracking and identity systems, including security alert signals to the nearest shore-based authorities in case a vessel is threatened, on all ships of 500 gross tons and above on international voyages. The alert system is to consist of two buttons, one on the bridge and one elsewhere in the ship. When pressed, they do not sound an alarm on board; instead they let authorities on shore know the identity of the vessel, its precise location and the time. However, there is no corresponding requirement for governments or national authorities to install equipment ashore to receive the signals from ships although many leading trading nations have decided to do so;
- development of ship security plans for all vessels engaged in international commerce;
- appointing a ship security officer, who will be responsible for crew training, applying the ship security plan and coordinating with port security officers. However, there is no provision for formally certifying their competence;
- preparing and implementing port security plans after making port vulnerability assessments according to specified guidelines; and
- appointing a port security officer, along with compulsory security training for port workers.

These measures are to apply from July, 2004.[2]

US-driven Measures
After the terrorist attacks on the US in September 2001, a number of countries took steps to tighten maritime security, container shipments and their land links in the global supply chain. The measures included increased screening, boarding and inspection of ships; heightened surveillance of port facilities and maritime infrastructure; and enforcing exclusion zones around sensitive port areas and ships such as military vessels and cruise liners.

The US has tightened security for ships, ports and container cargo movements more than most other countries. The US has also insisted that its measures have to be adopted by other states and foreign companies if they want to continue to trade freely with the world's largest market. The US-led measures include the Container Security Initiative, or CSI, and the Customs-Trade Partnership against Terrorism, or C-TPAT, to enhance security throughout the supply chain.

CSI

The CSI, first announced in January 2002, was operational in at least 16 major seaports in Europe, Canada and Asia by the end of 2003. Most of the 20 leading mega-ports that ship cargo containers to the US are in Asia and Europe. The 16 ports where CSI was deployed included: Rotterdam, Holland; LeHavre, France; Bremehaven and Hamburg, Germany; Antwerp, Belgium; Yokohama, Japan; Goteborg, Sweden; Felixstowe, Britain; Genoa and La Spezia, Italy; Vancouver, Montreal and Halifax, Canada; Pusan, South Korea; Singapore; and Hong Kong.

The aim of the programme is to identify and check a relatively small number of cargo containers for possible weapons of mass destruction or dangerous radioactive substances that terrorists might try to place inside any one of the more than 230 million standard steel boxes criss-crossing the globe each year by sea. The checking of suspect cargo bound for the US is done at foreign ports, before the containers are shipped to America.

To help with the identification and screening, small teams of officers from the US Customs and Border Protection agency within the Department of Homeland Security are stationed in participating foreign ports. The US has offered CSI members reciprocal checking rights in its ports. Both Japan and Canada have taken up the offer, so that containers bound for Japan and Canada by sea from the US are selectively screened.

As a result of the programme, US officials say that checks of sea containers increased to 5.2 per cent of total arrivals by September 2003, from 2 per cent two years earlier.[3]

CSI Core Parts

The CSI programme has several core parts: first, using intelligence and computer data banks to profile and identify high-risk cargo. For example, cargo from a country known to harbor terrorists could raise a warning flag. So could containers with odd routings or suspicious manifests — the documents supposed to list their contents.

A second core part of the CSI programme is to use gamma ray and x-ray imaging systems to screen suspect containers at the earliest possible point on their journey to the US. This non-invasive screening usually takes just a few minutes. Only if something odd is spotted is a container opened and the contents physically inspected.

A third core part of the CSI program is to develop more secure containers so that once they are packed and locked, they can be tracked electronically and their contents monitored throughout their journey to the point of unpacking. The objective, of course, is to prevent tampering and alert authorities in case it happens.[4]

CSI Phases One and Two

Phase one of CSI is focused on implementing the programme at the 20 foreign ports that ship 68 per cent of all the sea cargo containers entering the US. The governments of countries in which 19 of the 20 top ports are located have agreed to participate in CSI, including several major ports in China. Kioshiung in Taiwan was expected to become the last of the top 20 ports to join the CSI by the first half of 2004.

China's agreement in September 2003 to join the CSI and allow US customs inspectors into its ports was very significant and paved the way for the Washington and Beijing to sign a maritime agreement in December 2003 based on free trade and open market principles. More containers move between China and the US than any other nation in the world, with over 3.2 million shipped between the two each year. Nearly 32 per cent of America's total annual container sea cargo moves between the two countries.

Meanwhile, phase two of CSI is underway to expand it to other ports that ship substantial amounts of cargo to the US and have the infrastructure and technology in place to take part in the programme. The governments of Malaysia, Sri Lanka, South Africa and Sweden have already joined phase two of CSI and the US plans to enlarge the programme to include ports in the Middle East such as Dubai, Latin America, and in at least 11 additional European ports, including Gioia Tauro, Livorno and Naples in Italy.

Once phase two of CSI becomes fully operational, approximately 80 per cent of the 7 million sea cargo containers shipped to the US each year will be covered.[5]

C-TPAT

The CSI encompasses the seaborne leg of a container's journey to the point at which it leaves the landing port. The Customs-Trade

Partnership Against Terrorism, or C-TPAT, aims to secure other parts of the global supply chain, including sea and air cargo moving on land from its point of loading and to its point of unloading.

So far, over 4,000 companies are enrolled in C-TPAT, not only US importers, but also all major air, sea, rail and trucking carriers, a large number of brokers and forwarders, as well as domestic port and terminal operators. In August 2003, the US opened C-TPAT for the first time to foreign manufacturers — initially to those based in Mexico but subsequently to a select group located in other parts of the world.[6]

The 24-hour Rule

Since February 2003, the US has also insisted that detailed and accurate cargo declarations must be submitted to American customs authorities 24 hours before a container is to be loaded onto a vessel bound for the US. Before that, US Customs would accept information in a final bill of lading up to 30 days after a shipment's arrival in the US.

Meanwhile, the European Union is set to adopt a different 24-hour rule. It will require that cargo information be provided to EU customs authorities 24 hours before the goods arrive in the EU, not 24 hours before loading in the country of export.[7]

Europe Joins In

The European Commission, indicated in June 2003 that it had finally found a common approach to container security with the US, after months of dispute with eight of its fifteen members as well as the US government. The eight — Holland, Belgium, France, Germany, Italy, Britain, Spain and Sweden — had agreed to participate in the US-led CSI. The container traffic from their ports to the US covered approximately 85 per cent of all containers shipped from Europe to America.

The EC had launched legal action, called an infringement proceeding, against its eight members, arguing that the EU, not individual member states, had authority over customs agreements with countries outside the EU. The EC also complained that the bilateral CSI deals between America and the eight EU member states effectively gave cargo passing through the participating ports preferential treatment, and that shippers would divert US-bound goods to those ports from others in the EU, creating unfair competition.

US officials said that the terrorist threat was urgent and that there was no time to negotiate a deal with the EU, a notoriously bureaucratic and slow-moving behemoth. The eight EU states that joined the CSI insisted that they had the right to determine national policy. The EC said its aim was to ensure that all EU members applied the same security-related customs controls and that container traffic was not diverted.

Whether it was a case of the EC bowing to the inevitable or not, it signed an agreement in November 2003 to include container and supply chain security within the existing 1997 EU-US agreement on customs cooperation and mutual assistance. The EC said that a joint working group would meet promptly to work out the technical details of the accord. And, in a significant enlargement of the scope of the CSI, the EC said that the agreement would ensure not only the security of container cargo trade between the EU and the US but also the security of containers from all locations that are imported into, trans-shipped through, or transit the EU and the US. The US Mission to the EU said that the joint working group would address issues related to the expansion of the CSI to all 15 members of the EU and the 10 pending new members, as well as other matters related to container security.[8]

APEC

In Asia and the Pacific, the Asia Pacific Economic Cooperation forum (APEC) is being used by the US and other members of the group concerned about the economic and trade impacts of terrorism to keep countries in the region focused on securing commerce. This is significant because the 21 economies in APEC account for about 60 per cent of the world's GDP and half of its trade.

At their summit in Mexico in 2002, APEC leaders agreed on measures to improve security of trade and prevent money laundering for terrorist or other purposes. At their annual meeting in Thailand in October 2003, they expanded APEC's role in combating terrorism by deciding, among other things, to establish a regional trade and financial security initiative at the Asian Development Bank in Manila. This facility, the first of its kind at a multilateral development bank, will enhance security at seaports and in the cargo container trade as well as at airports.

APEC has been active in promoting its 2002 Secure Trade in the APEC Region (STAR) programme, holding a series of seminars and conferences to publicize the new multilateral and bilateral maritime security measures and encourage all APEC economies to adopt them in a timely and coordinated manner.[9]

Costs

The OECD estimates that new maritime and supply chain security measures will require an initial investment by the shipping and port industry and its users of at least US$1.3 billion, and will increase operating costs by US$730 million dollars per year thereafter. This estimate of global costs may be conservative but most officials and private sector executives involved in the shipping and cargo container industries agree that while security is expensive, insecurity could be even more expensive.

The US Coast Guard has said that the cost of implementing tighter security measures in US ports is about US$1.5 billion dollars in the first year and US$7.3 billion dollars over 10 years. The American Association of Port Authorities said in late 2003 that Congress has appropriated only US$513 million since the September 2001 terrorists attacks to help cover these costs.[10]

Compliance and Deadline Difficulties

The costs of complying with the new IMO and US rules are mainly in delays to shipments, added security staff or security-related work, and installing security equipment. For some shippers, shipowners and port authorities, the added costs have become a significant concern. Contentious issues include who will pay for the enhanced security, how costs will be shared between governments and the private sector, and the extent to which they will be passed on to consumers.

The problems in complying with the new maritime security rules surfaced graphically in the US itself at the end of 2003, when nearly half the nation's ships and about 80 per cent of its ports, ferry terminals and fuel-chemical tank farms failed to meet a 31 December deadline for submitting plans showing how they would deal with terrorism threats. It is obvious that security measures to prevent attacks on the US from the sea are lagging well behind moves to protect airports and planes since September 2001. US Coast Guard officials said that the deadline for submitting the plans was met by about 5,200 of 10,000 ships told to submit them and only 1,100 of 5,000 port facilities — despite potential heavy fines for laggards.

The Association of American Port Authorities said that one reason ships, ports and other maritime facilities had missed the deadline was because they were given too little time. The US government did not finalize what it wanted until 22 October 2003, after the industry had been told it would have six months to submit the security plans. They have to be implemented by 1 July 2004, when the Coast Guard can start banning ships and shutting ports that do not comply.

The IMO has told shipowners that they must implement the IMO's security measures in 2004 or face severe restrictions on their movements. Tankers, cargo ships, cruise liners and other large vessels travelling to foreign destinations must obtain the IMO's International Ship and Port Facility Security certificate by 1 July 2004 or they will no longer be admitted into foreign ports. By November 2003, only a small fraction of the world's 46,000 ocean-going ships had got their certificates. The price tag for the changes mandated by the IMO is put at between US$30,000 and US$60,000 per vessel, but owners have no choice if they want to continue operating after mid-2004. The IMO insists that it will not extend the deadline.

These new security measures, combined with an assertion of port state control, will put enormous pressure on all ships and ports that are involved in international trade to comply with the standards set by the IMO and powerful trading nations or blocs such as the US and the European Union. Failure by a port to comply with the security standards by 1 July 2004 will allow other countries to delay or bar vessels which visited that port. The US Coast Guard has warned that it will expect statements of compliance for the last 10 ports visited by any ship wanting to dock in the US. The costs for non-compliers, whether ports or ships, could be high. For example, many Caribbean nations say they will not be able to meet the standards in time. As a result, they could face severe restrictions in their US$20 billion seaborne trade with the US. Their inability to pay for the needed improvements could benefit China as the Caribbean loses its main competitive edge — the short time it takes to ship to the US.

The OECD Maritime Transport Committee has a study underway to assess the risks faced in various links of the sea–land transport chain, the potential cost of measures to counter those risks, and who should bear the costs. In a separate study, the OECD is looking at how to verify the identity of cargoes loaded for transport and how to prevent containers being tampered with en route. The goal is to ensure the integrity of container cargoes throughout their journey, from loading to final destination. The World Customs Union resolved in June 2002 to take a series of steps to protect the international trade supply chain from acts of terrorism or other criminal activities and established a task force of customs experts to implement them.

Governments and the private sector in Europe, the Asia-Pacific region and elsewhere say that they seek a balance between tighter maritime security and the efficient flow of trade. Some Asian governments have warned that their sovereignty and jurisdiction must not be reduced or compromised by CSI and other anti-terrorist measures being advocated by the US and other Western nations. But despite such concerns, all the major Asian trading economies have joined or agreed to join the CSI.[11]

Pressures to Join CSI

Goods arriving in the US by sea from foreign ports that are not in the CSI can expect to be delayed for at least two or three days while they are inspected. They may not be allowed into the US at all in future unless they come via a trans-shipment hub port that is CSI-compliant. Either way, this will be extremely costly for exporters to the US from non-CSI countries. Non-participants in C-TPAT will also face greater scrutiny and delays when shipping to the US. Participants in both programmes stand to gain a competitive advantage over non-participants.

The threat of differential treatment between CSI and non-CSI ports has been one of the main factors behind the decision of countries like Malaysia, Sri Lanka, Sweden and South Africa that are not among the 20 leading shipment ports to the US to sign on to the CSI programme.

Likewise, large shippers have been quick to seek C-TPAT validation from American customs for their supply chain security to expedite their US-bound shipments. Smaller ports and some small shippers have complained, saying that they cannot afford to compete with CSI and C-TPAT participants and that their shipments will be penalized as a result of their non-participation.

Still, this is clearly the intent of both US schemes — to get maximum effective compliance. And the strategy is working.[13]

Compliance Benefits

There will be offsetting benefits for those who comply with US security requirements. The benefits, which can amount to significant savings, should include faster processing when containers reach US ports, lower insurance costs and fewer losses due to theft.

The new security measures, when effectively applied and extended on a more universal basis, could help streamline global commerce as well as giving it greater protection. The security requirements will make it more difficult to falsify identification of goods for customs declaration purposes. This will reduce the scope for corruption and cut transaction costs.

For example, estimated losses from cargo theft worldwide range from US$30 billion per year to as high as US$50 billion. Most of the thefts involve cargo containers being transported by trucks. However, seaports and container staging areas are also prone to container cargo theft. The installation of container scanners in the Port of Rotterdam cost 15 million euros. But in one year, their use generated 88 million euros in customs and tax revenue that would otherwise have been lost, even though only 2 per cent of containers, on average, are subjected to checks in the port.[13]

Technology Innovation

One of the greatest potential benefits of both CSI and C-TPAT is the technology innovation they are spurring as governments and the private sector, increasingly in collaboration, seek new ways to overcome problems raised by fears of terrorism. A global seaborne transport system and supply chain network that are made more secure by advanced technology would be an enormous boon to trade, business and job creation.

Many companies are involved in efforts to develop and introduce a new generation of IT-enabled "smart and secure" containers that can be tracked remotely at all times when loaded. Such containers will have electronic seals, as well as physical locking systems, to prevent unauthorized opening. They will also contain sensors to detect explosive, radioactive, and harmful chemical or biological substances. This should ensure much better security from the point at which the container is loaded and shut to the point at which it is unloaded.

Multinational companies and other trade-reliant firms have a vested interest in hastening this result because they do not want any interruption in the supply chain that would keep their goods out of world markets and cost them money.

For example, leading port operators and shippers have banded together in the Strategic Council for Security Technology to develop the world's largest wireless cargo container tracking system. It operates in over 45 countries and 700 locations. Meanwhile, Hewlett-Packard, the computer and IT equipment manufacturer, is working on its own systems to ensure that its cargo is secure. The aim is not just to create new technologies but to make better use of existing ones by integrating them. The company is testing an electronic system to make sure the bill of lading matches a container's cargo by checking and rechecking manifests electronically at various points along the journey.

The US government is unlikely to set a timeline to force the US shipping industry to adopt any particular technology to meet the requirements of the CSI. Instead, the industry-wide retrofit will probably be incremental and not be dictated by official fiat. The US Department of Transportation is working with the Department of Homeland Security to test new technologies, such as radio frequency identification (RFID) tags and ultra-wideband communications systems for container tracking.

But more than two years after the terrorist attacks on the US, the two departments had not settled on the standards that a smart container should have. They were still debating whether it should provide a complete electronic manifest on the contents or whether that data should be maintained in back-end systems operated by the shipping companies. US supermarket chain, Wal-Mart Stores Inc, for example, has decided to install RFID tags down to the package level in its supply chain so that every item in the container can be checked.[14]

7 How Secure?

So how secure is global maritime trade and the inter-linked supply chain on land? It is clear that before the September 11 terrorist attacks on the US, there were gaping vulnerabilities not just in aviation security but in maritime and land transport security as well.

Since then, the international community has started to take action to improve the situation, especially for ships and ports that are major players in global trade. But progress has been patchy. Some companies and countries are moving faster and more effectively than others. And some of the laggards complain that they cannot afford the new security measures. Steps are being taken by the international community, spurred by the US, to ensure the integrity of containerized cargo at sea and on land. But given the scale of maritime trade and the even vaster scale of commerce moving through the global supply chain using cargo containers, the task is far from complete.

The US Customs and Border Protection Commissioner Raymond Bonner admitted as much when he told a US Senate Committee in September 2003 that although good progress had been made in implementing the Container Security Initiative in major international ports in Asia, Europe and Canada, "we still have much work to do to get CSI fully operational".

Accurate and timely intelligence of any terrorist threat is the key to success. Those looking for signs of weapons of mass destruction or radiological substances among the many millions of containers moving around the world carrying legitimate cargo are checking for the proverbial needle in the haystack. And they are under pressure to do so without unnecessarily slowing global trade or increasing its cost.[1]

The ABC Affair

The good news is that there has not been a terrorist attack involving the movement of cargo containers around the world, on sea or on land. But in September 2003, ABC News claimed to have exposed a crucial weakness in America's port security system by shipping depleted uranium to Los Angeles in a container from Jakarta in late July — a week before the terrorist bombing of the Marriott Hotel in the Indonesian capital that killed 12 people and wounded scores more. Depleted uranium metal is used in armour-piercing anti-tank rockets. But it cannot be used to make a nuclear weapon. Indeed importing depleted uranium into the US is legal; only the failure to declare it is not.

Nevertheless, the undeclared shipment appeared to raise some disturbing questions about maritime and supply chain security. The 15 pounds (6.8 kilograms) cylinder of depleted uranium, which is about the size of a soda can, was encased in a steel pipe with lead lining to suppress the material's radioactive signature. It was then packed in a specially padded suitcase that was placed in a teak trunk along with other furniture put into a container in Jakarta for shipment to the US.

The first question is how — in a country such as Indonesia with extensive connections to the Al-Qaeda and JI network — was an odd suitcase put into the container with no checks being made as to why it was there? Indonesia is not a CSI participant. ABC News says it took only a few days in Jakarta to find a shipper willing to send a container to America with almost no questions asked. The shipment was handled by Maersk Logistics, part of the giant Maersk shipping company, based in Copenhagen, Denmark.

According to ABC News, Maersk company officials said that their procedures did not require their agents to inspect containers loaded outside their pier area. Maersk provided what it called "door-to-door service", which allowed the container to be loaded at a furniture store, and that it relied on screening by Indonesian government officials to validate the shipping contents. One good thing to come out of the episode is that Maersk said that the ABC News findings had led it to investigate and review its procedures overseas.

The container with the depleted uranium departed Jakarta in a feeder vessel for the Malaysian port of Tanjong Pelapas where it was loaded onto a Maersk container ship. Malaysia had not yet joined the CSI, so there was no screening of the container before it was put onto the Maersk ship. In Singapore, the next port of call and a

CSI member, the container simply stayed on the ship while other boxes were loaded. So it was not checked in Singapore either.

The depleted uranium arrived at the Port of Los Angeles on 23 August, 2003. Because the container had come from Jakarta, it was targeted for screening by US Customs and Border Protection agents using hand-held radiation pagers and X-ray scanners. The container was cleared because nothing suspicious or harmful was detected and it left the port on 2 September.

US Customs insists that the screening system worked as it should because depleted uranium is not dangerous and does not emit the same radioactive signals as highly enriched uranium used in nuclear weapons. Yet Tom Cochran, a nuclear physicist at the Natural Resources Defense Council in the US, which lent the depleted uranium to ABC News for the venture, says that the highly enriched uranium used for nuclear weapons would, with slightly thicker (one third of a centimeter) lead shielding, give off a signature similar to depleted uranium in the screening devices that were being used by homeland security officials at American ports. If the depleted uranium cylinder had been highly enriched uranium, 15 pounds are sufficient to construct a 1-kiloton nuclear device with an explosive power equal to 1,000 tons of TNT. This is small on the scale of nuclear weapons but could still do a lot of damage in an urban setting.

On the other hand, a crude terrorist nuclear bomb made of highly enriched uranium or plutonium would probably weigh at least a ton and be larger and less well shielded than compact modern weapons, increasing the chance that authorites could detect and, hopefully, defuse it.

This technical, but important, debate begs the question why the depleted uranium encased in a steel pipe with lead lining was not picked up by the X-ray scanner in the Port of Los Angeles as a potential pipe or suitcase bomb and the container opened for a physical check.[2]

The State of Play

What the depleted uranium episode and other evidence in this book suggests is that maritime and container cargo security has moved from a position of extreme vulnerablity to terrorist abuse in 2001, to one of semi-vulnerability while new counter-terrorist measures are implemented and bedded down and more powerful and effective technology is applied to thwart terrorist infiltration or attacks.

Radiation detectors and X-ray machines at major ports in North America, Europe, Asia, and Australia and New Zealand are good and getting better. But they are not foolproof and only a small minority of containers are actually scanned.

This period of semi-vulnerability could last for at least several more years if — as appears likely — not all companies and countries move with the same speed or effectiveness to tighten security at ports, on ships and in the global container cargo supply chain. Overall security will only be as good as the weakest link in the chain.

Lax Ship Regulation

Counter-terrorism and law enforcement authorities trying to stop weapons of mass destruction from getting into the hands of countries and terrorist organizations that want to acquire them face a major problem. International shipping is so vast and so unevenly regulated that seagoing vessels owned by governments or their agents, or interests with criminal or terrorist aims, can easily find the flag of another state under which to operate.

To operate internationally, vessels must be listed in a recognized ship register of a country, which will then allow the vessel to fly its flag. In effect, the state of registration will then become the ship's "flag state". The flag state's obligations and responsibilities towards ships carrying its flag are set out in the United Nations Convention on the Law of the Sea (UNCLOS). All registers are supposed to check and control the safety standards and working conditions of vessels on their books. Some open flag registers — like most traditional national registers for ships — are well run and maintain high or adequate standards. But others fall well short of the norms needed to maintain maritime-related security in an age of weapons of mass destruction and increasing international terrorism.[3]

Criminal and Terrorist Havens

Global seaborne trade is intensely competitive. To cut costs, many shipowners have taken their vessels off national registers and put them on open registers. At least 40 states around the world, most of them developing countries, sanction open registers, or flags of convenience, as a way of making money. These nations rent their flags to shipowners of any nationality; some do not even have access to the sea. Land-locked Mongolia, for example, opened a register in March 2003 in Singapore, one of the world's busiest seaports. Land-locked Bolivia, too, has a register for foreign ships. Flags of convenience generally provide greater anonymity as well as tax benefits and lower costs than national registers.

Flags of convenience emerged in the 1920s, when US shipowners started flying the Panamanian flag to avoid US laws then in effect that prohibited the manufacture, import or sale of alcoholic beverages. The subsequent spread of flag registers to places such as Liberia and Cyprus was encouraged by shipping companies eager to find homeports in countries with low taxes and wages, as well as light regulation. Today, the main flag of convenience fleets in terms of gross tonnage belong to Panama, Liberia, the Bahamas, Malta, Cyprus, the Marshall Islands in the Pacific, and Saint Vincent and the Grenadines in the Caribbean. However, many of the smaller, newer flag states — such as Cambodia and Tonga — have had some of the fastest rates of growth and some of the worst records for criminal and terrorist connections. A surge of newcomers to the flag of convenience industry in the 1990s brought some register standards to new lows.

The flag of convenience registers compete for business. Some offer quick and cheap ship registration, often on-line at the click of a button, with few questions asked. As a result, terrorists and as well as those who smuggle arms, drugs, people and contraband can thrive in the poorly regulated havens which the flag of convenience system provides.[4]

Decline of National Registers

Nearly half the global shipping fleet by tonnage, 48 per cent in 2003, sails under flags of convenience, according to the International Transport Workers' Federation (ITF), including the majority of large tankers, bulk carriers and cruise liners. In the eleven years to 2001, flags of convenience more than doubled their share of container shipping to just over 43 per cent, from slightly more than 21 per cent in 1990.

Ships flagged in the European Union fell by 37 per cent in the ten years to 1995. Just over 13 per cent of the world's shipping now sails under the flag of an EU member state, down from 32 per cent in 1970. Why? Because many ships formerly on registers in Western countries and Japan, and on other well-managed but relatively expensive national registers, have shifted to open or foreign flag registers to minimize tax and other costs. Morover in some cases, the real owners of the vessels want to make themselves as anonymous as possible, and not always for fiscal or liability reasons. Terrorists can see the attractions of opaque ownership in shipping and have often used it to camouflage their activities.[5]

Mask of Corporate Ownership

To guard against a serious terrorist crime involving a ship, law enforcement authorities need to find out who actually owns the vessel and controls its movements and operations. Real, or beneficial, ownership is not just disguised by the widespread practice of putting ships on foreign registers. The long-established tradition of having companies, not individuals, own ships also makes checking ownership, for security reasons, difficult. The practice can justified in commercial terms: individuals naturally want to avoid personal liability for any accidents their ships may have. But the practice of making the registered owner or owners of a ship no more than a "brass plate" corporation provides an almost impenetrable cloak of anonymity.

Open, or flag-of-convenience, registers — which by definition do not have any nationality requirements — are the easiest places in which to register vessels that are covered by complex legal and corporate arrangements. But it is not so much the registers themselves that enable reclusive owners to hide their identities; it is the corporate arrangements that are widely and legally available in many countries to hide the ultimate owners, even if they are terrorists.[6]

The OECD Maritime Transport Committee is studying the various ways in which a cloak of secrecy can be created around the ownership of vessels. It will then identify best practices that would enhance transparency without breaching the confidentiality of commercially sensitive, but non-security-related, information.[7]

Most open registers do not require audited accounts from the shipping companies that use them, including some of the largest registers, among them Panama, Liberia, Bahamas and Belize. A number do not reveal the names of shareholders or directors, as in Liberia, Bahamas and Belize. It is easy and inexpensive for the beneficial, or actual, owner to hide behind a string of companies. Bearer shares — which, as the phrase suggests, can be passed from one individual to another and carry ownership rights — are allowed in many of the countries that offer open registers. Secrecy in the name of business confidentiality is the norm in the flag of convenience system.[8]

The US argues that even though its domestic laws permit "brass plate" corporations to own ships, the use of this device to hide the identity of terrorist organizations that threaten the safety and security of ships, ports and people cannot be justified on any basis. In the US itself, the US government has the authority to require detailed ownership information through all corporate layers to ensure that vessels registered in the US comply with US documentation laws. The aim is to find out who actually controls the movements or operations of the ship, or who derives profits from its trade.

The US insists that a flag state must provide a port state (meaning the country where the vessel is calling) accurate and complete ownership information for maritime security purposes if requested. Washington has proposed that the IMO develop international standards so that, in cases where there are reasonable grounds for suspecting terrorist connections, the identity of the person or entity in actual control of the vessel can be speedily made known to authorized security personnel. It suggests that such standards should make clear that the person providing the information, i.e., the captain of the vessel, the agent or owner, must provide a complete and accurate account, and that the port state will continue to apply domestic law in its internal waters in cases of false reporting, meaning that sanctions and legal penalties can be imposed.

The US acknowledges that complex issues are involved. But it says that there is precedent for flexible interpretation of ownership and control in the International Customs Convention on Containers of 1972. This convention avoids defining the "owner" of a container. Instead, it places the onus for ensuring security on the operator — the person who, whether or not the owner of the container, has effective control of its use.[9]

Flag State Operators

The Seafarers International Research Centre (SIRC) at Cardiff University spent three years researching and analysing the regulatory capacity of 37 states that offer shipping flags, including national flags and open registers. Mongolia and Bolivia were not among them. Nor were Tonga and Tuvalu, two small Pacific island-nations whose ships have gained notoriety in recent years for their alleged connection to Al-Qaeda-linked smuggling or the trafficking of materials related to weapons of mass destruction.

The Centre's flag state audit released early in 2003, found that the Danish Second Register (DIS), the German Second Register (GIS), Kerguelen Islands, Netherlands, the Norwegian Second Register (NIS), Norway, the Philippines and Britain all had a "high" capacity to regulate the vessels on their registers. In the second category, rated as "good" performers, were Bermuda, Canary Islands, Cayman Islands, Cyprus, Estonia, Hong Kong, Isle of Man, Latvia, Madeira, Netherlands Antilles, Russia, Singapore, Turkey and Ukraine.

The audit concluded that Antigua and Barbuda, the Bahamas, Barbados, Belize, Bolivia, Equatorial Guinea, Honduras, Lebanon, Liberia, Malta, the Marshall Islands, Panama and Vanuatu had only a "modest" regulatory capacity. At the bottom of the list were Cambodia and St Vincent and the Grenadines which had a "poor" record.

Nik Winchester, one of the two SIRC researchers who carried out the study, said that a large number of open registers had failed to produce adeqate regulatory regimes to ensure the safe operation of vessels, safeguard labour standards and provide transparency of vessel ownership. He said that "super unregulated" registers, such as Cambodia and Equatorial Guinea, mopped up ships considered too risky by the more established open registers, such as Panama and Liberia, thus extending the working life of such ships to operate almost free of control. "In this market for flags, the profit motive and effective regulation compete, ultimately, to the detriment of the latter", Winchester added.[10]

Union Concerns

As of mid-2003, the ITF had branded 29 countries as flag of convenience operators for allegedly permitting sub-standard ships to fly their flags: Antigua and Barbuda, Bahamas, Barbados, Belize, Bermuda, Bolivia, Burma/Myanmar, Cambodia, Cayman Islands, Comoros, Cyprus, Equatorial Guinea, German International Ship Register (GIS), Gibralter, Honduras, Jamaica, Lebanon, Liberia, Malta, Marshall Islands, Mauritius, Mongolia, Netherlands Antilles, Panama, Sao Tome and Principe, St. Vincent and the Grenadines, Sri Lanka, Tonga and Vanuatu.

When declaring a ship register to be a flag of convenience, the ITF says it takes into account:

- the degree to which the flag state permits foreign-owned vessels, as distinct from national ships, to fly its flag;
- the ability and willingness of the authorities in that country to enforce international minimum social standards on its vessels, including respect for basic human and trade union rights, freedom of association and the right to collective bargaining with bona fide trade unions;

- the social record of that country: the ITF looks at the degree to which the country has ratified and enforces the conventions and recommendations of the ILO;
- the safety and environmental record of that country: the ITF considers the country's record in ratifying the conventions of the IMO and enforcing them by carrying out port state control inspections and detentions of ships that are not in compliance.

The ITF continues to monitor flag states closely and reviews those that might be designated flag of convenience operators each year. In 2002, three flag states were added to the ITF list: Comoros, Jamaica and Tonga. The same year, four flag states were removed from the list because they were no longer considered to be operating as flags of convenience: Aruba, Canary Islands, Cook Islands and Tuvalu. In 2003, Mongolia was declared a flag of convenience by the ITF which said it also appeared that Malaysia, Bangladesh and more Caribbean countries risked being put in the same category in the near future. The ITF represents nearly 600 transport trade unions in 136 countries covering around five million seafarers and other transport workers. It has been campaigning against flags of convenience for more than 50 years. The ITF asserts that many flag of convenience ships are badly maintained and older than the average age of the rest of the world fleet. It also says that in 2001, 63 per cent of all reported ship losses at sea, measured by tonnage, were accounted for by just 13 flag of convenience registers and that the five worst performers were Panama, Cyprus, St. Vincent and the Grenadines, Cambodia and Malta.[11]

Free at Sea — The Cambodian Register

The Cambodian register has been among the most notorious flag of convenience operations in recent years, so notorious that the government in Phnom Penh — under pressure from the US and the European Union — decided to withdraw the contract to run the register from the privately-owned Cambodia Shipping Corporation in August 2002 after a series of scandals involving some of the more than 1,600 Cambodian-flagged ships.

The extraordinary thing is that Cambodia was allowed for so long, even after the terrorist attacks on the US in September 2001, to base its register in Singapore — a country with a government that takes security very seriously indeed.[12]

In June 2002, French commandos boarded the Cambodian-registered freighter *Winner* in international waters in the Atlantic amid an exchange of gunfire that injured one of the 12 crew members. The troops seized more than one tonne of Colombian cocaine worth well over US$100 million in a cargo that was registered as scrap iron destined for Bilbao in Spain. Officials said that the raid was the result of a 15-months of surveillance involving American, French, Spanish and Greek authorities.[13]

But there was also an earlier terrorist connection to the Cambodian flag business that raised red warning flags in Western intelligence circles. In November, 2001, Irish customs officers found 20 million smuggled cigarettes on the *Maria M*, a Cambodian-registered freighter that arrived in Estonia supposedly carrying a cargo of timber. The cigarettes, concealed in the centre of bales of timber, were liable to tax amounting to about three million Irish pounds. They were the largest haul of smuggled tobacco ever seized in Ireland. Anti-terrorist officials said that the operation was organized by criminals with links to the Real IRA, a terrorist faction opposed the peace accord in Northern Ireland agreed to by the mainstream IRA, the Irish Republican Army.[14]

Until its contract was terminated by the Phnom Penh government, the Cambodian register based in Singapore was operated by the Cambodia Shipping Corp. It claimed to have been appointed by the Cambodian government in 1994 as the exclusive agent to register ships under the Cambodian flag. The register in Singapore opened for business in 1995 and soon attracted hundreds of ships with its offer of low fees and a 24-hour service that promised to complete the processing of applications within an hour on the strength of faxed documentation alone. From June, 2000, the Singapore office offered on-line ship registration. After its reactivation as an open, instead of national register, the number of vessels flying the Cambodian flag rose to 564, from just 16 in 1995. Of the 564 ships, just over 70 per cent were reported to be owned and controlled outside Cambodia.[15]

South Korean and US intelligence agencies had been concerned about an official North Korean connection to the Cambodia Shipping Corp., through a senior North Korean diplomat who was stationed for many years in Phnom Penh and was one of the founding investors in the company. Intelligence agencies had noted the inclusion of at least a dozen North Korean vessels among ships that flew the Cambodian flag. A South Korean analyst said that such ships were suspected of smuggling North Korean ballistic missiles and components to Pakistan, Iran and Iraq and other countries in the Middle East. Indeed, the *So San*, an unflagged freighter from North

Korea that was found to be carrying Scud missiles to Yemen under sacks of cement after it was stopped and inspected in the Indian Ocean by Spanish and US forces in December 2002, may well have been the *Song Sang*, a North Korean-owned freighter on the Cambodian register, but with the last two letters of the first word and the last letter of the second word freshly painted over on the hull in an effort to avoid identification.[16]

Ships flying the Cambodian flag were also involved in numerous sinkings and collisions in which dozens of crew members were lost at sea, feared drowned. Between 1995 and 2002, at least 25 Cambodian-registered vessels were wrecked or stranded, and the register's fleet was involved in 41 recorded collisions and nine fires. Forty-five of its vessels were detained for various offences. So many Cambodian-flagged ships were detained in ports around the world for failing to maintain adequate safety standards and other abuses that the flag was blacklisted under the Paris Memorandum of Understanding on Port State Control, which rated the Cambodian register as "very high risk".

The Paris MOU consists of 19 port state administrations in Europe, Scandinavia and Canada which aim to eliminate the operation of sub-standard ships through a harmonized system of control and information exchange. Similar arrangements exist for the Asia-Pacific region (through the Tokyo MOU), Latin America (Vina del Mar), the Mediterranean and the Caribbean. Each year, the Paris MOU issues a blacklist of flag states whose vessels are at very high risk of being detained for poor safety standards. The Paris MOU compiled figures that showed vessels with the Cambodian flag accounted for 8.5 per cent of the 561 port detentions in the first four months of 2002, up from 2.5 per cent of 697 detentions in the same period of 2001. Statistics kept by the Tokyo MOU showed that the Cambodian flag accounted for 14.7 per cent of the 332 port detentions in the first four months of 2002, a slight improvement on the 18.6 per cent of the 332 vessels detained by states in the MOU in the same period of 2001.[17] Following an investigation into the *Winner* scandal, the Cambodian government announced in August 2002 that control of the Cambodian ship register would be taken over by Cambodia's Ministry of Public Works and Transport. However, in January 2003, the government awarded a new contract to South Korea's Cosmos Group, prompting a protest from the ITF.

The ITF General Secretary David Cockroft said that appointing another foreign contractor to run the register showed Cambodia had learned nothing and the government might well be putting the reputation of the country once again in the hands of another unaccountable offshore company. He added that Cambodia's only chance of cleaning up its register was to slim it down to ships flying a genuine national flag of Cambodia.[18]

The Tongan Register

In May 2002, the Privy Council of Tonga, a small Pacific island-nation run as a monarchy, announced that it would close its international ship register after repeated evidence that vessels flying the Tongan flag were involved in arms and people smuggling, some of which were linked to Al-Qaeda. An office had begun operating in Greece in 2000 and emerged as one of fastest-growing foreign flag of convenience registers in the world by attracting nearly 200 ships to sign on.

US officials investigated a shipping company named Nova — incorporated in the state of Delaware in the US and in Romania — after two of its Tongan-flagged vessels were used to smuggle suspected Al-Qaeda operatives into Europe. In February 2001, eight Pakistani men fled from one of Nova's freighters, the *Twillinger*, after it arrived in the Italian port of Trieste from Cairo. They falsely claimed to be crewmen and carried large sums of money as well as false identification. US officials say the men were sent by Al-Qaeda. With the help of Romanian intelligence, US officials began an investigation of the firm and a search for its ships (according to accounts by the Romanian newspaper *Ziua* that European officials confirmed).

In August 2001, the captain of another of Nova's Tongan-registered freighters, the recently renamed *Sara*, radioed to maritime authorities in Italy that 15 Pakistani men whom the ship's owner had forced him to take aboard in Casablanca, Morocco, were menacing his crew. The 15 claimed to be crewmen when questioned by US and Italian naval officers, but the captain said they knew nothing about seafaring. US officials say they found tens of thousands of dollars, false documents, maps of Italian cities and evidence tying them to Al-Qaeda members in Europe. The conclusion: that they, like the eight on the *Twillinger*, were possibly on a terrorist mission. The 15 were charged in Italy with conspiracy to engage in terrorist acts.

In January 2002, the Tongan-flagged *Karine A* was seized by Israeli naval commandos in the Red Sea with a cargo of Iranian-made weapons, including 50 tons of anti-tank missiles, mortars, machine guns, landmines and surface-to-surface rockets. Israeli authorities said that the arms were destined for Palestinian-controlled territory for use against Israel. Two months later, another vessel flying the Tongan flag, *Fanourious*, packed with 126 clandestine immigrants, was escorted into the port of Sicily by an Italian naval vessel after the rusty merchant ship put out a distress call. The crew was arrested for aiding an illegal operation. In March 2002, a cargo vessel, the *Monica*, also Tongan-flagged, was apprehended by the Italian navy after it arrived off the coast of Sicily carrying 928 people, reportedly Kurds from Iraq seeking asylum. The ITF found that in the 15 years before it ran foul of the Italian authorities, the *Monica* appeared to have been registered under no less than seven different flags of convenience: Sao Tome & Principe, Belize, Equatorial Guinea, Cambodia, Honduras, Malta and Tonga.

Italy's secret services say that they see increasing evidence that terrorist groups like Al-Qaeda are moving into the smuggling of illegal immigrants, a multibillion dollar trade they can use for funnelling operatives and funding other activities. An intelligence report released in September 2003, said that terrorist networks and groups who trafficked in illegal immigrants shared a natural overlap, often relying on false documents and intricate logistics, transport and communication arrangements. "There is the fear, too, that the same routes used for illegal immigration are being used by militants to help form Islamic terrorist groups", said the report, compiled by an agency that coordinates the work of Italy's secret services.

After announcing that its register would close because it was tarnishing Tonga's reputation, the Tongan government said in June 2002 that the 185 vessels on the register had been given 12 months' notice of termination. A Tongan official said that it was unlikely the country would get back into the business of flagging foreign ships. However, the ITF says that while the Tongan register has been closed to new entries, the Tongan government is honouring existing contracts. Like Cambodia and a number of other flag of convenience countries, Tonga had subcontracted its register to a private company that was not based there — Tonga's shipping register operated out of the Athens port of Piraeus.[19]

8 Proliferation Security Initiative

It is against this background of significant crime and lax regulation in international shipping — and the industry's vulnerability to abuse by terrorists — that US President George Bush launched the Proliferation Security Initiative (PSI) on 31 May 2003. Variously referred to as a compact or political arrangement, it is a programme of pre-emptive interdiction designed to intercept illicit exports related to weapons of mass destruction (WMD) anywhere in the world, whether by sea, air or land.

The definition of WMD encompasses nuclear, chemical and biological arms, related materials and associated delivery systems. The latter would evidently include a ballistic missile linked to a WMD warhead, but not a missile to carry a conventional explosive charge. The PSI is a response to the growing concern that countries or criminal organizations hostile to America will pass WMD-related materials to terrorists who may use them to attack the US, its allies or friendly countries around the world.[1]

The PSI is intended to build on and reinforce existing arms control treaties and multilateral arrangements, as well as national export controls on sensitive materials, including "dual use" items that can be used for legitimate civilian industrial purposes or for WMDs. The PSI aims to stop trafficking in WMD-related materials between "rogue" states and terrorist groups that its members feel pose the most immediate threat to global and regional security. North Korea and Iran are primary sources of proliferation concern to PSI members, according to US officials.[2]

The Nuclear Nonproliferation Treaty

There are five countries that are accorded international legitimacy as nuclear-weapon states under the Nuclear Nonproliferation Treaty (NPT), that entered into force in 1970. They are the US, Britain,

France, Russia and China. Three of the five — the US, Britain and France — are founder members of the PSI. The other two — China and Russia — are more ambiguous in their attitude to the PSI. But neither opposes the programme and each is prepared to give it some support. These five nuclear weapon states are important because they are also the five permanent members of the United Nations Security Council with the right to veto Council decisions.

Three other countries — Israel, India and Pakistan — are known to possess nuclear weapons. They have never joined the NPT. If they were to do so now, they would be treated as non-nuclear-weapon states and have to disarm because the treaty restricts nuclear-weapon status to nations that manufactured and exploded a nuclear explosive device before 1 January 1967.

North Korea, which the CIA suspects may have several crude nuclear bombs, announced its withdrawal from the NPT in January 2003. US officials indicate that compared to North Korea and Iran — an NPT member Washington has accused of cheating on its obligations by having a clandestine programme to develop nuclear weapons — Israel, India and even Pakistan are of lesser concern as would-be proliferators. Indeed, their cooperation is being sought in enforcing PSI activities.[3]

North Korea

North Korea appears to have been the main target of PSI interceptions so far. It is estimated to have earned about US$1 billion in legal exports in 2002, including textiles and seafood. But North Korea is believed to have earned at least that much annually in the past by exporting counterfeit US dollars and drugs like heroin and methamphetamines, all of which are illegal, as well as ballistic missiles and components, most of which are legal. Western officials allege that North Korea exports arms, drugs and illegal counterfeit money to pay for its nuclear and missile development programme, prop up the embattled regime of North Korean leader Kim Jong-il and prevent the North Korean economy from complete collapse.

Nuclear Wal-Mart

When the eleven original PSI members — Australia, France, Germany, Italy, Japan, the Netherlands, Poland, Portugal, Spain, Britain and the US — held their fifth meeting, in Washington, on 16 and 17 December 2003, they were joined by five additional participants: Canada, Denmark, Norway, Turkey and Singapore. Only three Asia-Pacific nations have so far joined the PSI — Australia, Japan and Singapore. The PSI aims to expand its reach by getting cooperation from countries that have large shipping fleets and those whose ports and waters are suspected of being used by shippers of WMD-related goods. The PSI is seeking new members among coastal states in Asia and the Middle East, notably India which has a strong navy and lies close to the busy sealanes between East Asia and the Persian Gulf. US officials say that more than 50 countries have signalled that they support the PSI and are ready to take part in interdiction efforts, most of which are expected to be within national jurisdiction and the result of better exchanges of intelligence and tighter export controls. Under UNCLOS, national jurisdiction includes coastal state sovereignty over the territorial sea which extends 12 nautical miles out from the coast.

PSI members want to increase the number of countries joining or working with them to deter or intercept not just WMD-related shipments that go by sea, but any by land or air as well. Of course, this is difficult. Many of the suspect items also have legitimate civilian uses. And some, such as the plutonium core of a nuclear weapon, may not be much bigger than a football. China, Russia and South Korea — as immediate neighbours that share land borders with North Korea — are important in this context. For example, North Korea has exported ballistic missiles and related technology to Iran and Pakistan by air and sea. The key air routes for Pyongyong — between North Korea and Iran and between North Korea and Pakistan — are through Chinese airspace.[5] France and Germany are working with the US on the PSI notwithstanding their differences with America over Iraq. Since the PSI group first met in Madrid in June 2003, members have agreed to review relevant laws and improve intelligence exchanges on suspected international transactions involving WMD-related materials.

They have also agreed to hold a series of sea, air and land interception training exercises stretching into 2004 in Europe, the Middle East and Asia. The first was held in the Coral Sea off the northeast coast of Australia in September 2003. It involved ships, patrol aircraft and helicopters from Australia, the US, Japan and France tracking, boarding and inspecting a freighter carrying chemical weapon precursors. In October, Britain hosted the first PSI air interception training session, a table-top simulation of how to intercept an aircraft suspected of transporting WMD. Then over the next few weeks, Spain and France separately hosted maritime interdiction exercises in the Mediterranean Sea.

The aim of these exercises and the moves to improve intelligence-sharing and expand participation in the PSI is to create a web of counter-proliferation partnerships that deter and impede trafficking in WMD-related materials.[6]

PSI Weakness

A major weakness of the Proliferation Security Initiative is its limited authority under international law. The US and its PSI partners are working to rectify this so that they can interdict shipments of WMDs to or from states with nuclear ambitions, or between states of proliferation concern and terrorist groups, where such shipments are taking place beyond the sea, air and land jurisdiction of the PSI countries.

For example, at the International Maritime Organisation, the US has tabled amendments to the 1988 Convention on the Suppression of Unlawful Acts Against the Safety of Maritime Navigation, the SUA Convention, so that it will cover terrorist crimes at sea, including using ships as weapons or to carry weapons of mass destruction or related materials. At present, only if the flag state expressly consents can foreign warships halt a ship flying that flag in international waters — except in the case of a few "universal crimes" such as piracy, slavery and unauthorized broadcasting. The US and its allies want the WMD terrorist threat put into a similar pariah category.

The US proposed to the IMO that if PSI countries want to board a ship carrying suspected terrorists or WMD-related material on the high seas, they should try to contact the flag state but if no response is received within four hours it will be taken as consent to stop and search the vessel.[7]

Liberian Breakthrough

In February 2004, the US and Liberia announced that they had agreed to new boarding and inspection arrangements on the high seas where either side has reasonable grounds to suspect that one of their ships is carrying WMD-related materials or items of proliferation concern.

Measured by gross tonnage, Liberia has more shipping flying its flag than any other country in the world, except Panama. According to Liberian authorities, over 2,000 vessels are on the Liberian register, which is based in the US. Under the new agreement, the US could contact the register and request the right to board a suspect Liberian-flagged ships anywhere in international waters — and do so after waiting no more than two hours for a response. In other words, no reply by then is to be taken as approval for boarding. The US regards this arrangement as a model for similar agreements it is pursuing with a number of other key flag states. After Liberia, the major shipping registers Washington is approaching probably include Panama, Bahamas, Greece, Malta, Cyprus, China, Hong Kong, the Marshall Islands, Russia, South Korea and Saint Vincent and the Grenadines.[8]

The British government, another founding member of the PSI, announced not long after the US deal with Liberia had been made public that it, too, was negotiating agreements with the world's biggest flag states for the right to search ships suspected of WMD trafficking on the high seas. Britain said it wanted to sign agreements with the world's 10 largest shipping nations covering some 70 per cent of global maritime trade.

Making the announcement to the British Parliament, Foreign Secretary Jack Straw said that alongside its partners, Britain was considering whether to introduce new penalties to deter shipping and air lines from seeking to move WMD cargoes. "Might the vessels and planes of any companies found to have engaged in such transport be denied landing or port rights around the world? Should we consider an international register of companies and individuals convicted of proliferation offences?" he said in his written statement to parliament.[9]

WMD-related Interceptions and the Nuclear Merry-go-round
Well before the new high seas search plan was announced by the US and Britain, PSI members were taking pre-emptive action wherever they were able to do so legally.

In April 2003, shortly before President Bush formally announced the PSI, French authorities, acting on a German government tip-off, ordered a French cargo container ship, the *Ville de Virgo*, to unload suspicious cargo in an Egyptian port. Originating from a German firm in Hamburg, the cargo included 214 ultra-strong aluminium pipes weighing 22 metric tons purchased by China's Shenyang Aircraft Corp. The cargo was cleared by German customs agents but hours after the ship left Hamburg, German intelligence officials discovered that the aluminium was destined not for China but for North Korea. The intended use of the pipes, they concluded, was not for making aircraft fuel tanks, but as key components of advanced centrifuges for making highly-enriched uranium for nuclear weapons.

On 12 April 2003, in a dramatic but little-noticed intervention, French and German authorities tracked the Asia-bound container ship to the eastern Mediterranean and seized the pipes. German police arrested the owner of a small export company and uncovered a broader scheme by North Korea to acquire as many as 2,000 such pipes. That much aluminium could have yielded as many as 3,500 gas centrifuges for enriching uranium. One option, since the *Ville de Virgo* was French-owned and technically under France's jurisdiction, was to stop it at sea and transfer the suspect cargo to a French military vessel. Instead, it was decided that the pipes should be unloaded at the first possible port. The ship's French owner endorsed the plan. The captain then made an unscheduled stop in the Egyptian port of Alexandria, not far from the northern entrance to the Suez Canal. The pipes were quickly and quietly removed and another vessel returned them to Hamburg on April 28.[10]

French and German authorities also collaborated in the first half of 2003 to intercept sodium cyanide that was thought to be bound for North Korea's chemical weapons programme.[11]

Japan Tightens Up

Japan, a long-time source for high-tech parts for missiles and nuclear weapons for North Korea, has also stepped up its crackdown on the illicit trade. In April 2003, a trading company in Tokyo associated with a pro-Pyongyang group of ethnic Koreans in Japan attempted to export devices that could be used to make missiles and nuclear weapons to North Korea via Thailand. The devices, which control electric currents that can be used for enriching uranium, were reportedly seized in Hong Kong when the freighter stopped there on its way to North Korea. Japanese officials alerted authorities in Hong Kong that the transformers were being shipped under false documentation.[12]

Later in 2003, Japan sharply increased its searches of North Korean ships calling at Japanese ports and Japanese police arrested five executives from a used-car dealership for exporting a huge trailer to North Korea that could be used to move a missile launch pad.[13] Japan also convened an export control policy meeting of eight Asian states in Tokyo in October 2003. Senior officials from Japan, the United States, China, South Korea, Australia, Singapore, Thailand and Hong Kong took part. Participating countries agreed to tighten their controls over exports of materials that could be used to develop weapons of mass destruction and intensify the exchange of timely intelligence about suspected trafficking in WMD-related materials, including to or from North Korea. They agreed to set up a system through which they could inform each other about suspected shipments of such materials to North Korea via third countries. It is the first time that an arrangement for multilateral cooperation in export control over strategically sensitive items as been put in place in Asia.[14]

In December 2003, Japan said that it planned to tighten its own rules on the export of products and parts that could be used in weapons of mass destruction, and might offer aid to other nations to enable them to do the same. The rules are not specifically aimed at North Korea but a Japanese trade ministry official said that it is one nation being kept in mind. The new rules will expand the list of products whose export is limited out of concern they could be used for WMD or the missiles that could carry them. Currently, some 30 products, including gyroscopes, fall into this category. Japan is also considering providing money from its overseas development assistance to Asian nations such as Indonesia, the Philippines and Vietnam to enable them to tighten their export controls in the same area, starting in March 2004.[15]

PSI Seizures

In August 2003, in response to a US request, Taiwanese officials confiscated about 150 barrels of phosphorus pentasulphide from a North Korean freighter, *Be Gae Bong*, in the Taiwanese port of Kaohsiung before it left for North Korea. The chemical is used to make insecticide and as an additive in motor oil. But it can also be used to manufacture nerve gas.[16]

But the most important PSI seizure made public so far was the interception by German and Italian authorities in October 2003 of the *BBC China*, a German-owned ship, after it passed through the Suez Canal bound for Libya. In Dubai, equipment that could be used to enrich uranium for nuclear weapons had been loaded onto the ship. Labelling on the packing cases showed that the sophisticated components had been precision-made at a factory in Malaysia, which claimed later it thought the equipment was for the oil industry. The parts had been identified and tracked by US and British intelligence.

US officials say that the interception of the Libya-bound shipment helped convince the Libyan government to agree not long afterwards to abandon its WMD programme under international supervision. The confiscated equipment from the ship also helped investigators to unravel and shut down the Pakistan-based nuclear black market headed by Abdul Qadir Khan.[17]

China and PSI

China's attitude to the PSI could be crucial to its success or failure. John Bolton, the US Undersecretary of State for arms control and international security, said in November 2003 that China supported the concept behind the PSI and was prepared to engage in joint activities to curb WMD trafficking. Russia, he said, had no objection to engaging in WMD interdiction activities.[18]

Still, China is in a bind. As host of the six-party talks to end the nuclear stand-off on the Korean peninsula, it does not want to appear to be provoking or isolating North Korea by taking part in any blockade. The six-party talks involve North and South Korea, the US, Russia and Japan as well as China. If China, Russia and South Korea were to join or cooperate openly with PSI members, it would range five of the six parties in the talks against North Korea. Pyongyang sees the PSI as an alliance to enforce a blockade to bring North Korea to its knees.[19]

However, China also has a pressing national security interest in a nuclear-free Korea and has said repeatedly that it wants the whole peninsula to be free of nuclear weapons. Without stable borders and a peaceful neighbourhood, China will not be able to focus fully on expanding and modernizing its economy. "A developing China needs both an international and peripheral environment of long-term peace and stability", said a non-proliferation "White Paper" published by the Chinese government in December 2003. "The proliferation of WMD and their means of delivery benefits neither world peace and stability nor China's own security".[20]

A Chinese foreign ministry spokesman said two days after the White Paper was released that China understood the WMD concerns of PSI members but was also mindful of concerns about the legitimacy, effectiveness and impact of the methods the group would use to intercept suspect shipments. Still, the spokesman said that China would take the proliferation risk into full consideration when exporting sensitive items and technologies to other countries.[21]

The US said that China had enacted a good piece of legislation, although it needed to be implemented and enforced. Significantly, however, the US Secretary of State Colin Powell had disclosed in

November 2003 that Beijing had cooperated with the US to block some chemicals leaving China for North Korea. This was the first reported case of such cooperation in an arms control area that had previously been a source of chronic tension between the US and China. The CIA had told the US Congress in January 2003 that North Korea had continued to procure raw materials and components for its ballistic missile programmes from various foreign sources, especially through North Korean firms based in China. "We are pleased with China's recent cooperation with us to block the export of chemicals that could have been used in North Korea's weapons programs", Mr Powell said. "And our very success in that particular case has now set a much higher standard for our cooperation." He added that neither America nor China wanted to see weapons of mass destruction spread and "by acting on that mutual interest, China can turn the issue of proliferation from a negative to a positive in our relations".[22]

With the cuts in US and Japanese aid to North Korea, China is by far the largest supplier of fuel oil and food to the North, giving it a degree of leverage that other countries do not have. Beijing's confirmation in September 2003 that its military have taken over from police in guarding the 1,400-kilometre border with North Korea may well be a ratcheting up of Chinese pressure on Pyongyang, short of working with the PSI group of nations. South Korea and Russia, too, are likely to refrain from open cooperation with the PSI, at least until they are convinced that North Korea will not dismantle its nuclear weapons programme.[23]

North Korea's *Pong Su*

In April 2003, Australian special forces boarded and took control of a North Korean freighter in Australian waters that was involved in an attempt to smuggle into Australia 125 kilograms of heroin with a street value of up to AUD$200 million. US and Australian officials suspect that North Korea uses profits from state-sponsored smuggling of drugs, arms and counterfeit money to help pay for its programmes to develop weapons of mass destruction.

Although not strictly within the ambit of the PSI, Australia worked closely with the US and Japan to track and investigate the 4,000-ton *Pong Su*, which had travelled to Japan many times but was registered under a flag of convenience in the small Pacific island-nation of Tuvalu. The *Pong Su* was impounded in Australia. Its North Korean crew of 30, including a senior member of the ruling Korean Workers' Party who was on board when the ship was seized, are in detention in Australia until their court trial is held. It has been delayed, evidently because the Korean defendants have been reluctant to talk to Australian investigators. The North Korean government has denied any involvement with the ship or its cargo of heroin.

Some reports say that this operation was under a programme separate from the PSI, known as the DPRK Illicit Activities Initiative and that there has been a quiet crackdown by many countries against the narcotics trade, counterfeiting, money laundering and other efforts by the Democratic People's Republic of Korea to earn hard currency.[24]

North Korea's Flagless Missile-carrier

The legal and political complexities involved in intercepting ships in international waters, particularly if they are owned or registered in countries that are not members or cooperating partners of the PSI, was illustrated late in 2002 when the US picked up intelligence from its spy satellites that North Korea was preparing an export shipment of Scud missiles. After tracking the suspect freighter from North Korea for several weeks, the US asked its NATO ally, Spain, to send a warship to halt, board and inspect the vessel in the Indian Ocean as it steamed towards the Middle East.

Under international law, warships can stop a foreign commercial vessel on the high seas only if they have permission from the flag state, if the vessel is "without nationality" or if it is reasonably suspected of piracy, carrying slaves or unauthorized broadcasting. The flag state is the government of the country whose flag the vessel to be intercepted is flying.

After the cargo ship was boarded and inspected, North Korea described the incident as an act of piracy. But US navy planes tracking the freighter found that the name on its hull read *So San*, in letters apparently freshly painted. Checks found that no ship named *So San* was registered. That provided grounds for treating it as "without nationality", meaning that it could be legally boarded.

The US had also observed that, in an apparent effort to obscure its identity and origins, the freighter was now sailing without a flag when it should have been flying the flag of the country where it was registered. This provided further legal grounds for boarding. Under international law, ships not properly registered, flagged or marked can be boarded. A US official said that in fact the freighter was a Cambodian vessel with a North Korean crew. The Spanish frigate sent to intercept the freighter ordered it to slow for boarding on

9 December 2002. But the demand was ignored despite two salvos of warning shots, a third salvo into its bow and sniper fire from Spanish special forces to clear cables blocking their way to board. After a six-hour standoff, they rapelled from a helicopter onto the deck and secured the freighter. A subsequent check of the cargo holds by American forces found crates containing 15 Scud missiles, 15 conventional warheads and many barrels of chemicals, all hidden under thousands of bags of cement.

But on 11 December, the US decided to let the freighter sail on to its destination. There was no clear legal basis for holding the missiles, and their purchaser was Yemen, an important ally of America's in the war on terrorism. The Yemeni government had protested against the ship's seizure and demanded its release, saying that the purchase contract for the extended range Scud B missiles had been signed a long time ago and that the Yemeni military needed them for defence purposes and would not transfer them to a third party.

Frustrated by the outcome and slow pace of anti-terrorist action at the UN, the Bush administration decided to launch the PSI using the "coalition of the willing" approach to try to choke off North Korea's WMD-related trade and fight weapons proliferation more broadly.[25]

9 Sea Change and Recommendations

Under international law, every ship must sail under the flag of a sovereign state to gain the protection of a government while on the high seas. A key lesson from the *So San* affair and other terrorism or WMD-related trafficking in international waters is that those trying to shut the trade down by pursuing suspect ships wherever they are need to get cooperation from the government whose flag the ships are flying. At present, only if the flag state expressly consents, can foreign warships legally halt and inspect a ship flying its flag on the high seas — except in a few specific cases, among them "universal crimes" such as piracy, slavery and unauthorized broadcasting. Because nearly half the world's fleet by tonnage is now on foreign registers, this means that, in many cases, permission to halt and inspect in international waters must be sought from a "flag-of-convenience" state.

As noted at the end of Chapter 8, the US and Britain have asked countries that operate or sanction foreign flag registers to cooperate in allowing boarding and search to take place when it is reasonably suspected that the ship involved is carrying WMD-related cargo to or from states or non-state actors of proliferation concern.

IMO and Reform

The International Maritime Organization's motto is: "safer shipping, cleaner seas". But the IMO shies away from using the term "flag of convenience", talking instead of sub-standard shipping. It has for some time been developing a voluntary model flag state audit that could be used to improve the regulation of global shipping and the fight against terrorism.

Progress was frustratingly slow until late 2002. It now appears that a voluntary scheme could be in place by mid-2005, followed by a mandatory one later. The new IMO Secretary-General Efthimios

Mitropoulos has said he is determined to ensure that the audit scheme is a success and has placed it under his direct supervision.[1]

The IMO has been slow in the past to improve its regulation of sub-standard shipping in part because leading operators of open registers — including Panama, Liberia, the Bahamas, Malta and Cyprus — are among the largest contributors to the IMO's regular budget. These countries are among the 29 that the ITF has listed as flag of convenience providers. Panama, Liberia, the Bahamas, Malta and Cyprus comprise five of the top ten contributors to the IMO budget. Together, the five accounted for almost 40 per cent of the assessed contributions to the IMO approved budget of £39.5 million for 2002–2003. Contributions to the IMO annual budget are based on a formula which is different to that used in other UN agencies: the amount paid by each member state depends primarily on the tonnage of its merchant fleet, not on its per capita GNP.[2]

One Way Forward

The ITF believes that only by reestablishing the full role and responsibilities of the flag state, and by ensuring that there is a genuine ownership and control link between a ship and the flag it flies, can effective maritime governance be achieved. Better regulation of shipping and cleaning up its sub-standard black spots are clearly crucial not just to the safety of the maritime industry and seaborne trade but to its security as well, especially when the risk of WMDs and dirty bombs getting into terrorist hands is rising.

Japan is an example of the potentially dangerous movement of ships from national to open or flag of convenience registers. After Greece, Japan owns more commercial ships than any other country: nearly 14 per cent of the world total, measured in deadweight tonnage in January 2002. Yet only 793 of Japan's nearly 3,000 ships remain on the Japanese national register. In terms of the deadweight tonnage of vessels owned by Japan, over 86 per cent were registered under a foreign flag of convenience in 2002. Some 43 per cent of Japanese-owned ships fly the flag of Panama, 7 per cent the flag of Liberia, and 1 per cent each the flags of Bahamas, Malta and Cyprus.

With so much of the Japanese commercial fleet on foreign registers and manned by non-Japanese crews, it is quite possible that a ship domiciled in Japan and owned by a Japanese company but flying a flag of convenience could be leased or time-chartered to a front firm for a terrorist organization without the Japanese authorities being in a position to know anything about it — even if the ship were to be used to carry a nuclear or radiological bomb into a major Japanese port.

It is, however, possible to reverse the flow of ships to foreign registers and bring them back to national registers. Singapore has shown how tax and other inducements can be used to rebuild a national register while meeting international maritime safety and labour standards. According to *Lloyd's List*, Singapore, with 1,768 ships, had the world's seventh largest merchant fleet by gross tonnage at the end of 2002, behind Panama, Liberia, Bahamas, Greece, Malta and Cyprus but ahead of Norway, China, Hong Kong, Marshall Islands, Japan, Russia, the US, Italy, Britain, Denmark, South Korea, St Vincent and the Grenadines, and Germany. Of the 717 ships domiciled in Singapore at the start of 2002, 455 were on the national register.[3] Only 34 per cent of the total deadweight tonnage of the Singapore fleet flew a foreign flag of covenience.[4]

Singapore's effort to attract quality vessels from reputable shipping companies to its national registry is paying off handsomely. In March 2004, AP Moeller, parent company of the world's biggest shipping group, Maersk Sealand, revealed that it would register 20 new vessels under the Singapore flag by 2007. They will include new crude oil and product carriers, car and truck "roll-on, roll-off" vessels, and seven of the largest container ships ever built. The latter are on order from South Korea's Hyundai Heavy Industries. AP Moeller said that more of its fleet might be registered in Singapore in future.

The commitment represented a 61 per cent increase in the Danish group's Singapore fleet of 33 vessels. According to the Maritime and Port Authority of Singapore (MAPA), 3,065 vessels totalling 25.4 million tons were on the Singapore register by early 2004. MAPA has sent delegations overseas to encourage shipowners to register their fleets in Singapore. The island-state has for more than decade sought to position itself as an international maritime centre by offering a full range of shipping industry facilities and services. AP Moeller indicated that its decision to put 20 of its most modern ships under the Singapore flag had been influenced by the Singapore authorities' business-friendly policy towards shipping.

In its March 2004 budget, the Singapore government cut corporate tax by 2 per cent, to 20 per cent, and expanded tax exemptions for onshore chartering income for shipping companies that fall under its Approved International Shipping Enterprise (AIS) scheme. The AIS, launched in the early 1990s, provides international shipping firms that base regional operations in

Singapore with 10-year renewable tax-exempt status over most earnings, provided they flag at least 10 per cent of their fleet in Singapore and spend a minimum of S$4 million (US$2.4 million) per year in the island-state.[5]

There is debate over the distinguishing features of "open", "national", or "international" registers. UNCTAD, notes that in six big and six smaller open, or flag of convenience registers it has studied, the share of tonnage *owned by nationals of these open-registry countries* is minimal, well below 10 per cent.

However, UNCTAD says that a similar study it made of eight international registers, including Singapore, showed two hallmarks. First, nationals of the country or territory of the registry have a substantial share of the tonnage registered, as is the case with Singapore, Hong Kong, Denmark and Norway. Second, nationals of a country having a privileged relationship with the territory of registry have a significant share of the tonnage registered, as in the case of Britain with the Isle of Man registry, the US with the Marshall Islands registry, France with the French Antarctic Territory (the Kerguelen Islands) registry and the Netherlands with the Netherlands Antilles registry. In these international registers, the share of tonnage owned by nationals or by citizens of countries having a privileged relationship with the territory of registry is high — well above 30 per cent and in some cases over 80 per cent.[6]

Reputable Shipowners Act

Meanwhile, international shipowners' organizations have for the first time issued guidelines for measuring the performance of states that register ships under flags of convenience against their legal obligations. The Roundtable of International Maritime Organisations says the guidelines will encourage flag states to improve their performance. They include a list of 12 countries that score a dozen or more negative indicators. Flag states branded as poor performers include Albania, Belize, Bolivia, Cambodia, Costa Rica, the Democratic Republic of Congo, Honduras, Jordan, Madagascar, Sao Tome and Principe, Suriname and Syria.

"Ship operators may wish to consider carefully whether the use of flags that have a large number of negative performance indicators is in the interest of either the company or the industry at large", the guidelines say. They point out that shipping companies may face higher numbers of port inspections and expensive delays if they fly the flag of a suspect state.[7]

Unions Urge Port State Pressure

Seafaring unions linked to the ITF have urged the US Congress to enact legislation authorizing the US Coast Guard to refuse entry to American ports to any non-US flagged ship that does not provide full identity of the vessel's actual owner or owners.[8]

Safety to Security

Until quite recently, port state concerns — even in countries like the US which face an acute terrorist threat — have focused on *safety, rather than security*. Reform of shipping practices considered substandard by those responsible for protecting international maritime security and the global supply chain from terrorist attack is likely gain real traction when port states led by the US start delaying or turning away flag of convenience or other ships with known or suspected terrorist connections when the new IMO rules on ship security come into force from July 2004.

Conclusions and Recommendations

The most dangerous possibility in maritime terrorism — indeed it is a nightmare scenario for many officials and analysts in the West and Asia — is that terrorists might sooner or later obtain and use:

- a powerful radiological bomb, in which conventional explosives disperse deadly radioactive poison; or
- even a nuclear bomb, perhaps concealed in any one of the more than 230 million cargo containers that move through the world's ports each year.

But there are other risks. This summary highlights the following threats, listed in order of their potential to wreak havoc on world trade.

The Ultimate Doomsday Scenario

1) A nuclear weapon or bomb exploding in a port-city that is also a key node in the seaborne trading system and its land links to the global supply chain.

There are over 30 such mega port-cities spread over Asia, North America and Europe. They include:

- In Asia — Hong Kong, Singapore, Shanghai and Yantian in China, Kaohsiung in Taiwan, Tokyo and Yokohama in Japan, Pusan in South Korea, and Laem Chabang in Thailand.

- In the US — New York, Los Angeles, Long Beach, Charleston, Seattle, Norfolk, Houston, Oakland, Savannah and Miami.
- In Canada — Vancouver, Montreal and Halifax.
- In Europe — Antwerp in Belgium, Rotterdam in the Netherlands, Le Havre and Marseilles in France, London and Felixstowe in Britain, Bremerhaven and Hamburg in Germany, Genoa and La Spezia in Italy, Algeciras in Spain and Goteburg in Sweden.

Many of these mega port-cities are also the location of the top 20 container terminals. In 2002, the top 20 terminals were ranked in the following order of size: Hong Kong, Singapore, Pusan, Shanghai, Kaohsiung, Shenzhen, Rotterdam, Los Angeles, Hamburg, Antwerp, Long Beach which also serves Los Angeles, Port Klang in Malaysia, Dubai, New York, Quingdao in China, Bremenhaven, Gioia Tauro in Italy, Manila in the Philippines, Tokyo and Felixstowe. As the ships that carry containers on long voyages become larger to take advantage of economies of scale, many of the leading terminals act as trans-shipment points for smaller ships and regional ports in a hub-and-spoke system.

Seaborne trade is vulnerable to a well-planned terrorist attack on two fronts:

- the handful of international straits and canals through which 75 per cent of world maritime trade passes. These waterways are relatively narrow and could be blocked;
- the port-city hubs that form an interdependent global trading web and increasingly dominate container shipping. An ever greater proportion of container shipping trade is being concentrated in giant ports with the modern facilities to handle the boxes.

The Penultimate Doomsday Scenario
2) A radiological, or "dirty" bomb, exploding in one of these mega port-cities.

Third-level Doomsday Scenario
3) A terrorist attack or a coordinated series of strikes that did not use nuclear or radiological bombs but instead used ships as weapons to close one or more key international ports, straits or

waterways. The damage to world trade caused by such action would depend on how long the blockage lasted, the extent to which it could be bypassed, and the costs involved.

Impact on Global Trade

The detonation of either a nuclear or powerful radiological bomb in a major port-city would cut the arteries of maritime commerce if the device was believed to have come by sea. It would halt much of the world's trade and severely damage the global economy, as governments scrambled to put extra security measures in place to protect their populations, cities and economies.

Such measures would be drastic and include:

- lengthy cargo inspections in the ports of the affected country, as well as in ports of nations that did extensive sea trade with it; or
- the complete closure of ports for an indefinite period,

while additional checks and safeguards were implemented to allay public fears.

Impact on Insurance

What would happen to insurance rates if terrorists attacked, or worse still closed, a major port, strait or waterway used for international trade? Ship and cargo insurance rates would skyrocket. After terrorists set the *Limburg* ablaze off the Yemeni coast in October 2002, underwriters tripled premiums on ships calling at ports in Yemen. The exorbitant cost of insurance and the fear of further attacks made many vessels cut Yemen from their schedules or divert to ports in neighbouring states.

A nuclear or powerful radiological bomb attack on a major international port would send ship and cargo premiums to prohibitive levels. The bigger the attack up the scale of terrorist violence, the greater the insurance shock would be. There is no insurance for a maritime-related terrorist attack using a nuclear bomb. The recovery costs would be unimaginably huge. They would also be very heavy if a radiological bomb were detonated in a mega port-city. Whether private insurance payouts would be available to aid recovery from a dirty bomb explosion is doubtful.

Even a terrorist attack using a ship or ships to block one or more key international ports, straits or waterways — but not involving nuclear or radiological bombs — would trigger a damaging upward spiral in insurance rates and make many ships avoid the area.

Recommendations

A) Disaster Prevention

I. TIGHTEN SECURITY OVER NUCLEAR WEAPONS, AND
    FISSILE MATERIAL, RADIOACTIVE SUBSTANCES,
    EQUIPMENT AND TECHNOLOGY THAT COULD BE
    ACQUIRED BY TERRORISTS AND USED TO MAKE
    NUCLEAR OR RADIOLOGICAL BOMBS.

The US and other governments have established programmes to keep
fissionable materials for making nuclear bombs out of terrorists'
hands. In February 2004, US President George Bush announced
seven proposals to strengthen international efforts to stop the spread
of nuclear weapons and materials or technology that could be used
to make them. But clearly, more needs to be done by the nuclear
powers, in collaboration with the IAEA, to secure fissile material and
nuclear weapons. Just as urgent, although less well known, is the
threat from other radioactive substances that could easily find their
way into the hands of terrorists.

As already noted in this book, the IAEA has warned that the
radioactive substances needed to build a dirty bomb can be found
in almost any country in the world, and that more than 100
countries may have inadequate control and monitoring programmes
to prevent or even detect the theft of these materials.

This is an open invitation for terrorists and traffickers to move
in and get what they need to make radiological bombs; indeed, there
is evidence that they are seeking to do this. The IAEA needs more
support from UN member states, more money and more resources
to do its job effectively and prevent a dirty bomb being made and
used.

II. A UNIVERSAL CONTAINER INITIATIVE IS NEEDED TO
     SUPLEMENT THE US-DRIVEN CONTAINER SECURITY
     INITIATIVE AND PROVIDE BETTER SECURITY
     THROUGHOUT THE GLOBAL SUPPLY CHAIN TO
     PREVENT A NUCLEAR OR RADIOLOGICAL BOMB BEING
     PLACED IN A CONTAINER OR ON A SHIP INVOLVED IN
     INTERNATIONAL TRADE.

A container checking system similar to the CSI needs to be adopted
by all ports for all destinations that are significant links in the
seaborne supply chain powering the world economy. Both the US

and the EU appear to recognize the importance of expanding the coverage of the CSI. At present, *containers bound for the US* are the main focus of checks, although Canada and Japan have accepted a US offer to screen any suspect containers in American ports before they leave for Canada or Japan.

But the CSI system remains very US-oriented. In Singapore, for example, containers headed for the US and Singapore itself are checked if intelligence indicates there may be a problem. But containers from or trans-shipped through Singapore that are bound for the rest of the world are not screened, irrespective of where they come from.

The US and the EU agreed in November 2003 to work out ways of ensuring the security of containers from all locations that are imported into, trans-shipped through, or transiting the EU and the US. This would amount to a very large portion of the world's general cargo trade. Leading Asian traders should adopt a similar approach. This would be the genesis of a Universal Container Initiative.

The IMO and the World Customs Organization are the most appropriate multilateral forums for coordinating such a strategy. The OECD is studying how to ensure the integrity of seaborne container cargo throughout its journey, from the point on land where it is loaded and sealed in the container to the point where it is unloaded for delivery after the ocean voyage.

III. HARNESS TECHNOLOGY AND TAP THE PRIVATE SECTOR

It should be possible to implement a more universal system of container security over the next few years as new technology for "smart and secure" containers becomes widely available and costs come down. These IT-enabled containers will have satellite-communication connections so that they can be tracked remotely at all times when loaded. They will have electronic seals, as well as physical locking systems, to prevent unauthorized opening. They will also contain sensors to detect explosive, radioactive, and harmful chemical or biological substances. Non-invasive scanners using X-ray, gamma ray and other technologies will also improve.

Companies owning containers could be encouraged by tax incentives as well as government regulation to introduce the "smart and secure" containers.

IV. SECURITY MUST TAKE PRIORITY OVER SECRECY IN SHIPPING

Lifting the shroud of secrecy covering the ownership and control of ships, and improving seafarer recruitment and identification, are critically important in preventing terrorists from using ships for their own purposes. Failure to do so will mean that terrorists can work within, and under the cover of, the new maritime security arrangements that have already been applied or will be in place by the end of 2004.

Seafarers are to be issued biometric identification documents by their governments to guard against terrorist infiltration. To reinforce this, the IMO should develop a database of all seafarer certificates and work with its member-states to crack down on fake papers.

To guard against a serious terrorist crime involving a ship, law enforcement authorities may need to find out who actually owns the vessel and controls its movements and operations. Real, or beneficial, ownership is not only disguised by the widespread practice of putting ships on foreign registers. The long-established tradition of having companies, not individuals, own ships also makes checking ownership for security reasons difficult. The practice can be justified in commercial terms: individuals naturally want to avoid personal liability for any accidents their ships may have. But the practice of making the registered owner or owners of a ship no more than a "brass plate" corporation provides an almost impenetrable cloak of anonymity.

Open, or flag-of-convenience, registers — which by definition do not have any nationality requirements — are the easiest places in which to register vessels that are covered by complex legal and corporate arrangements. But it is not so much the registers themselves that enable reclusive owners to hide their identities; it is the corporate arrangements that are widely and legally available in many countries to shroud the ultimate owners in anonymity, even if they are terrorists.

The OECD Maritime Transport Committee is studying the various ways in which a cloak of secrecy can be created around the ownership of vessels. It will then identify best practices that would enhance transparency without breaching the confidentiality of commercially sensitive, but non-security-related, information.

Most open registers do not require audited accounts from the shipping companies that use them, including some of the largest registers, among them Panama, Liberia, Bahamas and Belize. A number do not reveal the names of shareholders or directors, as in Liberia,

Bahamas and Belize. It is easy and inexpensive for an owner to hide behind a string of companies. Bearer shares are allowed in many of the countries that offer open registers. Secrecy in the name of business confidentiality is the norm in the flag of convenience system.

The US argues that, even though its domestic laws permit "brass plate" corporations to own ships, the use of this device to hide the identity of terrorist organizations that threaten the safety and security of ships, ports and people cannot be justified on any basis. In the US itself, the government has the authority to require detailed ownership information through all corporate layers to ensure that vessels registered in the US comply with American documentation laws. The aim is to find out who actually controls the movements or operations of the ship, or who derives profits from its trade.

The US insists that a flag state must provide a port state (meaning the country where the vessel is calling) accurate and complete ownership information for maritime security purposes, if requested. Washington has proposed that the IMO develop international standards so that, in cases where there are reasonable grounds for suspecting terrorist connections, the identity of the person or entity in actual control of the vessel can be speedily made known to authorized security personnel. The US wants such standards to ensure that the person providing the information, i.e., the captain of the vessel, the agent or owner, provides a complete and accurate account, and that the port state will continue to apply domestic law in its internal waters in cases of false reporting, meaning that sanctions or legal penalties can be imposed.

The US acknowledges that complex issues are involved. But it says that there is precedent for flexible interpretation of ownership and control in the International Customs Convention on Containers of 1972. This convention avoids defining the "owner" of a container. Instead, it places the onus for ensuring security on the operator.

V. THE ULTIMATE SANCTION IS PORT STATE CONTROL AND IT SHOULD BE STRONGLY ASSERTED TO MAKE ALL SHIPS, PORTS AND COMPANIES COMPLY WITH THE NEW MARITIME SECURITY STANDARDS MANDATED BY THE IMO.

Many countries and companies, particularly the smaller and less affluent, complain of the difficulty and costs in meeting the new security standards. In some cases, financial aid and technical assistance may be warranted to make compliance possible for governments and ports in developing countries. Industrialized nations, and regional agencies such as APEC and the Asian

Development Bank, are already helping governments and ports in developing countries to raise their security levels to meet international standards and join the US-sponsored Container Security Initiative. More help may be needed on the basis that security is only as strong as the weakest link in the chain.

But the IMO should not extend its deadline for implementing its new standards, which in most cases must happen by 1 July 2004. Too much is at stake for world trade and global security for slippage to be tolerated. The fact is that most countries, ports and shipping lines with a major interest in seaborne commerce will comply, if they have not already done so, because the costs of non-compliance far outweigh the costs of conforming.

Until quite recently, port state concerns — even in countries like the US which face an acute terrorist threat — have focused on safety, rather than security. The new security measures, combined with an assertion of port state control, will put enormous pressure on all ships and ports that are involved in international trade to conform with the standards set by the IMO and powerful trading nations or blocs such as the US and the European Union.

The IMO has told shipowners that they must implement its security measures in 2004 or face severe restrictions on their movements. Tankers, cargo ships, cruise liners and other large vessels travelling to foreign destinations must obtain the IMO's International Ship and Port Facility Security certificate by 1 July or they will no longer be admitted into foreign ports.

Ships that do not pass the security tests will be liable to fines or exclusion. This will force sub-standard vessels to improve or become pariahs of the sea. Failure by a port to comply with the security standards by 1 July 2004 will allow other countries to delay or bar vessels which visited that port.

B) Disaster Recovery

I. SET UP AN INTERNATIONAL SYSTEM FOR DEFUSING A MASS TERROR BOMB OR COPING WITH THE AFTERMATH OF AN EXPLOSION.

Many countries have drawn up plans for managing a major terrorist attack on their ports and cities, although how effective they would be in coping with the mass panic following a radiological bombing, or the horrific devastation and casualties after a nuclear explosion, is open to question because they have never been activated to deal with such catastrophes. Industrialized nations and some other countries have emergency response units and proceedures in place to defuse a radiological or nuclear bomb found in their national jurisdiction before it explodes.

Given the impossibility of completely securing seaborne trade and the global container cargo supply chain, and given the growing risk that terrorists will resort to mass violence, possibly by using a dirty bomb on a ship or in a container, in or near a key port-city or international shipping strait, the five declared nuclear powers, (US, Britain, France, Russia and China), or as many of them as are prepared to act, should establish a mechanism for coordinating the prompt despatch of technical teams to help any country threatened by a terrorist weapon of mass destruction or a radiological bomb to neutralize it.

Since speedy action would be vital, three other known nuclear powers — India, Pakistan and Israel — should also be called upon to assist if necessary, based on their geographical proximity to the crisis point. The country in which a WMD or dirty bomb was found would need to request outside help if it was unable cope by itself. Such an assistance mechanism could be linked to the IEAA. If a WMD or dirty bomb exploded, the same channel through the IAEA could be used to coordinate the international assistance required to cope with the disaster and recover from it.

America has a special responsibility in this regard, since it has insisted that all containers arriving by sea in its huge market — the world's largest — be checked for WMD and dirty bomb materials in foreign ports. The US, which has a large reservoir of expertise and technical know-how to disarm nuclear and radiological bombs, calls the CSI a defence-in-depth strategy. In effect, however, it is foisting on other countries the potentially terrible consequences of mass terror aimed primarily at America.

Many of those countries do not have the resources and capacity of the US to defuse nuclear or radiological bombs or cope with the devastating aftermath if they explode. US policy on the CSI is an application of the "not-in-my-backyard" syndrome. It is perfectly understandable in the climate of terrorist threat that surrounds the US. But it will be seen, rightly, by many other countries as a policy of utter selfishness that is being enforced by the world's sole superpower unless it is accompanied by a readiness to help cope with the possible consequences.

II. THE MARITIME SUPPLY CHAIN NEEDS A "RESTART" MECHANISM IN CASE IT IS HIT BY AN ACT OF CATASTROPHIC TERRORISM.

This study concludes that if a nuclear or powerful radiological bomb was brought by sea into a major port-city or international shipping strait and exploded, it would halt or severely disrupt world trade. The global seaborne supply chain can probably never be made immune from this kind of attack. The fight against terrorism is likely to last for years. A key issue facing policy planners must therefore be how to build a global seaborne supply chain that is sufficiently resilient to withstand a devastating shock and resume operations quickly enough to avoid precipitating a world economic crisis.

How long would it take for port and shipping trade to get up and running again if a terrorist catasrophe happened? There are at present no agreed international arrangements for reviving the maritime supply chain system after a crisis; there is no "restart" button or mechanism. This is serious gap that needs to be filled. One way of doing so may be to add a security mandate to the work of the WTO, much in the way that the APEC forum has been given responsibility for promoting and facilitating secure trade in the APEC region.

Notes

Chapter 1: Trade, Terrorists, Shipping, and Cargo Containers

[1] "Screening Cargo for Terror Shipments", *International Herald Tribune* (IHT), 23 September 2003.

[2] Speech by Singapore's Deputy Prime Minister and Finance Minister Lee Hsien Loong, at the Jurong Shipyard National Day Observance Ceremony, 10 August 2002.

[3] Speech by Frits Bolkestein to Freight Forwarders, Brussels, 1 December 2003.

[4] Remarks by Singapore's Deputy Prime Minister Dr Tony Tan at the 2nd International Institute for Strategic Studies (IISS), IISS Asia Security Conference, Singapore: The Shangri-La Dialogue, 1 June 2003; World Trade Organisation (WTO). *World Trade Developments in 2002 and Prospects for 2003*, 5 November 2003 (Geneva: WTO), p. 2.

[5] WTO, op. cit., p. 4; OECD, "Security in Maritime Transport: Risk Factors and Economic Impact" (Paris: OECD), July 2003, p. 6; UNCTAD, "Review of Maritime Transport, 2003" (Geneva: UNCTAD), 7 November 2003, pp. 77–78.

　　The top 20 container terminals listed by UNCTAD, with their 2002 throughput (in millions of TEUs), are: Hong Kong (18.61), Singapore (16.94), Pusan (9.33), Shanghai (8.62), Kaoshiung (8.49), Shenzhen (7.61), Rotterdam (6.52), Los Angeles (6.11), Hamburg (5.37), Antwerp (4.78), Long Beach (4.52), Port Klang (4.53), Dubai (4.19), New York (3.75), Quingdao (3.10), Bremenhaven (3.03), Gioia Tauro (2.99), Manila (2.87), Tokyo (2.83), and Felixstowe (2.80).

[6] US Department of Energy, World Oil Transit Chokepoints, Country Analysis Brief, November 2002; British Petroleum (BP), Statistical Review of World Energy, June 2003, <http://www.bp.com/subsection.do?categoryId=95&contentId=2006480>.

[7] Tom Ridge, US Secretary of Homeland Security, Speech presented to the Institute of Defence and Strategic Studies, Singapore, 6 March 2004, p. 1.

[8] Jack Short, Secretary General of the European Conference of Ministers of Transport, speech to the Irish Exporters Association in Dublin, Ireland, 21 March 2003.

[9] Testimony of US Director of Central Intelligence Agency George J. Tenet, to the Senate Select Committee on Intelligence, 24 February 2004, "The Worldwide Threat 2004: Challenges in a Changing Global Context"; Mohamed ElBaradei, "Saving Ourselves from Self-Destruction", *New York Times*, 12 February 2004; Andrew Koch, "The Nuclear Network — Khanfessions of a Proliferator", *Jane's Defence Weekly*, 3 March 2004; "Terrorists have the Will to Use Dirty Bombs, US Officials Warns", Associated Press, 8 February 2004; Singapore's Defence Minister Teo Chee Hean, "Challenges to Security in the Asia-Pacific", Opening address to the Asia Pacific Security Conference, Suntec, Singapore, 22 February 2004, p. 2.

Rear Admiral Teo, a former chief of Singapore's navy, said that terrorism was the most immediate security threat facing countries across the globe. He added:

> The threat of terrorism is amplified by the risk of proliferation of weapons of mass destruction. The nightmare scenario of terrorists and rogue regimes collaborating in the use of weapons of mass destruction is now well within the realm of possibility. If terrorists were to set off a nuclear device or chemical or biological agents, the damage and panic would be massive.

[10] OECD, "Report on Ownership and Control of Ships", March 2003 (Paris: OECD).

[11] OECD, "Report on Security in Maritime Transport: Risk Factors and Economic Impact" (Paris: OECD, July 2003), p. 6; UNCTAD, "Review of Maritime Transport", 2003, op. cit., p. 3; US Department of Homeland Security, "CSI in Brief"; Robert Bonner, Commissioner of US Customs and Border Protection, Speech to the Heritage Foundation, Washington, D.C., 9 September 2003.

[12] OECD, "Report on Security in Maritime Transport", op. cit., pp. 23–27; UNCTAD, "Review of Maritime Transport"; "Special Report on Container Trade: When Trade and Security Clash", *Economist*, 4 April 2002.

[13] Australian Department of Foreign Affairs and Trade (DFAT), "The Costs of Maritime Terrorism and Piracy and the Benefits of Working Together", paper presented at the APEC High-level Meeting on Maritime Security and Cooperation, 8–9 September 2003, Manila; Danny Chan, Modern Maritime Threats and Strategies, paper presented to the Institute of Defence and Strategic Studies (IDSS), Singapore, 16 October 2003; RAND Europe, "'Seacurity': Improving

the Security of the Global Sea-Container Shipping System", 8 September 2003; Frits Bolkestein, op.cit., p. 2.

[14] European Community, Proposal to the European Parliament on Enhancing Port Security, 2 May 2003, p. 14.

[15] Australian Broadcasting Corporation, "How Safe are Our Borders", programme about the attacks on 11 September 2003, by Brian Ross, Rhonda Schwartz and David Scott.

[16] Greg B. Smith, *New York Daily News*, 22 August 2003.

[17] *North America Regulations Shipper*, 22 August 2003, posted on Containerisation International online, <www.ci-online.co.uk>, on the same date; CNN, 9 August 2003, "Pakistani in US Aided Al-Qaeda", by Phil Hirschkorn; and the Jang Group of Newspapers, Pakistan, 6 August 2003, "Uzair Paracha — FBI's New Scapegoat".

Jang reported from New York that

> ... authorities do not believe the company that employed Paracha is connected to Al-Qaeda or terrorism-related activities. They are also not certain if he was actually plotting attacks in the US or abroad, one source said.
>
> However, the source also said, authorities do believe Paracha may have been closely connected to Khalid Shaikh Mohammed, Usama bin Laden's senior operational commander. Mohammed, who was captured in Pakistan last spring, is suspected of having organised the September 11 (2001) terrorist attacks. US authorities also believe he smuggled or attempted to smuggle Al-Qaeda operatives into the United States even after the attacks.
>
> Meanwhile, Paracha's father, who also works in the shipping industry, is in US custody as well. Saifullah Paracha runs a clothing export business in Pakistan that ships goods to the United States.

[18] US Department of Justice, Federal Bureau of Investigation (FBI), press release, 8 October, 2003, "US Indicts Pakistani Man on Charges of Providing Support to Al-Qaeda".

The release states that "Paracha is accused of agreeing to help an Al-Qaeda associate obtain documents that would allow him to re-enter the United States and conduct financial transactions with the associate. To accomplish this, Paracha also agreed to pose as the associate while in the United States, and to take other actions to assist the Al-Qaeda associate."

[19] US Department of Justice, press release, 8 August 2003, "Statement of Attorney General Ashcroft regarding the filing of charges against Pakistani man for agreeing to assist an Al-Qaeda operative".

[20] Greg B. Smith, *New York Daily News*, 22 August 2003, and FBI criminal complaint filed before Judge Andrew J. Peck, Southern District of New York, on 8 August, 2003.

The complaint states that:

> Paracha is a citizen of the Pakistan with lawful permanent resident status in the United States. Paracha arrived in the United States most recently in mid-February 2003, and had been staying with relatives in Brooklyn.
>
> Paracha is employed by a business in New York, which also has an office in Karachi, Pakistan. Approximately two weeks before Paracha left Pakistan for the United States, Paracha met an individual whom he learned wanted Paracha to perform tasks for him in the United States. Paracha met this individual (hereinafter "CC-1") at the Karachi office of the business by by which Paracha is employed. CC-1 was with another person (hereinafter "Subject-1").
>
> Paracha was advised that CC-1 and Subject-1 wanted to invest approximately US$200,000 in the business for which Paracha worked in Karachi. Paracha was advised not to ask any questions about the money because CC-1 and Subject-1 were supporters of Usmama bin Laden. Paracha believed the funds to be Al-Qaeda money, and CC-1 and Subject-1 wanted to keep the funds liquid and to be able to retrieve them on short notice. Paracha believed that if Paracha did not perform the tasks that CC-1 was requesting him to undertake in the United States, then CC-1 and Subject-1 might not invest the money in the business.

[21] *United States of America v Uzair Paracha*, Defendant indictment, 8 October 2003.

[22] Ronni Berke, CNN, 9 October 2003, "Pakistani Faces More Terror Charges".

[23] Phil Hirschkorn, CBS news, 8 August 2003, "Qaeda Suspect Charged in New York", and CNN, 9 August 2003, "Pakistani in US Aided Al-Qaeda".

[24] Phil Hirschkorn, CNN, 14 October, 2003, "Lawyers Predict Another Moussaoui Case".

[25] OECD, "Report on Security in Maritime Transport", op. cit. pp. 7, 8; William Langewiesche, "Anarchy at Sea", *Atlantic Monthly*, September 2003, p. 64; Richard Owen and Daniel McGrory, "Terrorist in a Box", *Times* (UK), 25 October 2001; Andrea Felsted and Mark Odell, "Agencies Fear Extent of Al-Qaeda's Sea Network, *Financial Times*, 21 February 2002.

[26] *Economist*, Special Report on Container Trade, April 6, 2002.

[27] Niala Boodhoo, "Other Groups, with Al-Qaeda, Said to Threaten US", Reuters, 20 May 2002.

Chapter 2: Al-Qaeda's "Navy"

1 "Ship Searched after Al-Qaeda Tip", *New Zealand Herald*, 31 October 2003.

2 "South Korea on Alert for Possible Al-Qaeda Ship", Agence France-Presse (AFP), 30 October, 2003 and "No Al-Qaeda Clues on Ship", *New Zealand Herald*, 1 November 2003.

3 Martin Bright, Paul Harris and Nick Paton Walsh, "The Armada of Terror", *Observer*, 23 December 2001; "Agencies Fear Extent of Al-Qaeda's Sea Network".

4 John Mintz, "15 Freighters Believed to be Linked to Al-Qaeda", *Washington Post*, 31 December 2002. "This industry is a shadowy underworld", a senior US government official was quoted as saying in the article. "After 9/11, we suddenly learned how little we understood about commercial shipping. You can't swing a dead cat in the shipping business without hitting somebody with phony papers".

5 Peter Grier and Faye Bowers, "How Al-Qaeda Might Strike the US by Sea", *Christian Science Monitor*, 15 May 2003, and "Bin Laden's Navy", CBS news, 31 December 2002,

6 David Ensor, "Navy Ships Searching for Al-Qaeda in Arabian Sea", CNN, 7 December 2001; and Martin Bright et al., "The Armada of Terror", *Observer*, op. cit.

7 John Mintz, op. cit.; Andrea Felsted and Mark Odell, op. cit.

8 "Al-Qaeda Boats with Drugs Seized", AFP, AP and Reuters, *Straits Times*, 22 December 2003; "US Seizes Al-Qaeda Drugs Ship", BBC, 19 December 2003; "US Navy Seizes Al-Qaeda Smugglers Dhow", *Financial Times*, 20 December 2003; Ron Moreau and Sami Yousafzai, "A Deadly Habit", *Newsweek*, 14 July 2003; US State Department, 6 November 2002, "US Arrests Seven in Two Drugs-for-Weapons Deals".

9 NATO, press release, 17 November 2003, "Operation Active Endeavour"; NATO, press release, 31 July, "Nato Ships Start Boarding Operations In Mediterranean", NATO Regional Headquarters for Allied Forces Southern Europe.

10 Princeton N. Lyman and J. Stephen Morrison, "The Terrorist Threat in Africa", *Foreign Affairs*, Jan/Feb 2004; John S. Burnett, *Dangerous Waters: Modern Piracy and Terror on the High Seas* (New York: Plume 2002), p. 299; Emily Wax, "Kenya to Charge Four in Mombasa Bombing", *Washington Post*, 24 June 2003; James Macharia, "Islamic Preacher with Terror Mission on Kenya Coast", *Washington Post*, 3 March 2004.

11 Princeton N. Lyman and J. Stephen Morrison, "The Terrorist Threat in Africa", p. 2; Lt Joshua A. Frey, "NAVCENT Hosts Maritime Security Cooperation Conference", US Navy newsite <www.news.navy.mil>, 26 November 2003.

12 Admiral Thomas Fargo, chief of the US Pacific Command, Speech to the Homeland Security Conference, 21 November 2003, Hawaii.

13 US Department of Justice statement, 15 May 2003, "Al-Qaeda Associates Charged in Attack on USS Cole"; BBC, "Charges Filed for USS Cole Attack", 15 May 2003.

The BBC reported that a total of 50 counts of various terrorist offences were filed against two Yemeni fugitives, Jamal al-Badawi and Fahd al-Qusaa, who remain at large after escaping from a prison in Yeman with 10 others in April 2003. "Badawi and Qusaa are alleged to be longtime Al-Qaeda terrorist associates who were trained in the Al-Qaeda terrorist camps in Afghanistan in the 1990s", US Attorney General John Ashcroft told a news conference.

The Department of Justice said that the indictment named bin Laden as as an unindicted co-conspirator, saying that he had allegedly planned the attacks on the two US navy ships and later praised the suicide bombers. Bin Laden has been indicted by the US in connection with the 1998 bombings of two US embassies in East Africa that killed 250 people, among them 12 Americans.

14 CNN, 3 November 2000, "C-4 Quantity may be Clue in USS Cole Bombing"; CBS, 20 June 2001, "A Claim for the Cole"; CBS, 12 October 2001, "Chilling Anniversary for USS Cole"; CBS, 25 April 2002, "Homecoming for Ship-Shape Cole".

15 Karl Vick, "Crew Backs Suspicions of Attack on Oil Tanker", *Washington Post* report in the *International Herald Tribune* (IHT), October 11, 2002; CBS, 11 October 2002, "Was Tanker Target of Terrorist Attack?"; Bloomberg, 15 October 2002, "Yemen Attack may have been Remote-controlled Bombing".

16 Chris Tomlinson, "US said to Thwart Terror Attacks in Horn of Africa", Associated Press, 25 November 2003; "USS Cole Bombing Mastermind Nabbed in Yemen", *Straits Times*, 27 November 2003; "Yemen Pursuing Second Top Al-Qaeda Figure after Arrest of Cole Attack Mastermind", Associated Press, 26 November 2003; Zahid Hussain, "Al-Qaeda Leader is in Group of Six Men Arrested in Pakistan", *Asian Wall Street Journal* (AWSJ), 1 May 2003; CBS News, 3 April 2002, "Bin Laden Deputy Profiled"; "Kuwait Captures Leader of Tanker Bombing", *New York Times* (NYT), 18 November 2002.

17 US Department of Justice statement, 15 May 2003, "Al-Qaeda Associates Charged in Attack on USS Cole"; CBS News, 22 November 2002, "Suspected Qaeda Chief Cooperating."

18 Maki Becker with James Gordon Meek, "Terror Lurks on High Seas", *New York Daily News*, September 21, 2003; CBS News, 16 June 2002, "Bin Laden said behind Gibralter Plot".

19 CBS News, 22 November 2002, "Suspected Qaeda Chief Cooperating"; Fox News, 23 November 2002, "US Captures Al-Qaeda's Persian Gulf Chief".

20 Peter Finn, "Arrests Reveal Al-Qaeda Plans", *Washington Post*, 16 June 2002; CBS News, 16 June 2002, "Bin Laden said behind Gibralter Plot"; BBC, 21 February 2003, "Saudis Jailed for Al-Qaeda Plot."

21 Christopher Dickey, "High-Seas Terrorism", *Newsweek*, 27 January 2003.

22 CBS News, 22 November 2002, "Suspected Qaeda Chief Cooperating".

23 Charles R. Smith, "Al-Qaeda Plans Scuba Diver, One-man Submarine Attack", *Cyber Diver News Network*, 26 August 2003.

24 Stefano Ambrogi, "Iraq War could Spur Al-Qaeda Sea Attacks in Gulf", Reuters, 21 February 2003.

25 Sebastian Rotella, "Fears Persist of Al-Qaeda Terrorist Link to Dive Center", *Los Angeles Times*, 15 February 2003.

26 John Mintz, "US Fears Terrorists at Sea: Tracking Ships is Difficult", *Washington Post*, 31 December 2002; Maria Ressa, CNN, 23 October 2002, "Maritime Terror Attack Alert".

27 *Economist*, 4 October 2003, "Peril on the Sea."

28 Republic of Singapore Government, White Paper, "The Jemaah Islamiyah Arrests and the Threat of Terrorism", 7 January 2003, pp. 13, 27–30.

29 CNN, "Maritime Terror Attack Alert", op. cit.

30 BBC, 1 May 2003, "Pakistan Arrests USS Cole Suspect".

31 Zahid Hussain, "Al-Qaeda Leader is in Group of Six Men Arrested in Pakistan", *AWSJ*, 1 May 2003.

32 BBC, interview with Tanner Campbell, Vice-President of the Maritime Intelligence Group in Washington, D.C., The World Today, 22 January 2003; Vijay Sakhuja, "Terrorist Sea Strategy: the Kamikaze Approach", Peace Forum Essays, April 2003, Jawaharlal Nehru University, New Delhi.

33 Peter Chalk, "Liberation Tigers of Tamil Eeelam's (LTTE) International Organization and Operations — a Preliminary Analysis", Canadian Security Intelligence Service, Commentary no. 77, 17 March 2000, p. 9.

Writing well over 18 months before the devastating Al-Qaeda attacks on New York and Washington, Chalk, then an analyst for the

Rand Corporation in Washington, wrote prophetically that the LTTE's "international support network has ensured that the group is at the cutting edge of contemporary terrorist lethality and sophistication, possibly providing the prototype for the type of insurgent organization that the world is likely to witness in the next decade".

[34] *AWSJ*, 5 November 2003, "Sri Lankan Peace is Threatened"; Edward Luce, "Sri Lanka Crisis as President Fires Ministers," *Financial Times*, 6 November 2003; "President takes Extra Powers in Sri Lanka", *IHT*, 6 November 2003.

[35] Peter Chalk, op. cit.

[36] Peter Chalk, op. cit., pp. 5, 6.

[37] OECD, Report on Security in Maritime Transport, op. cit., pp. 14, 15.

[38] Chalk, op. cit., p. 8.

[39] *Sunday Times*, 27 June 1997, "Mortar Ship Mystery Still Baffles Defense Officials"; "Arms Ship Mystery Deepens, Possibility of LTTE Ploy: Zimbabwe Official Here for Probe", *Sunday Times*, 3 August 1997; "The Arms Trade", *NYT*, 7 March 1998; "A Tamil Tiger Primer on International Arms Bazaar", *IHT*, 10 March 1998.

[40] Australian Broadcasting Corporation, 2 March 2004, "Cambodia Announces Plans to Destroy its Obsolete Air Weapons Systems". This report noted that the US had launched a global drive to secure, or eliminate, what it calls Man Portable Air Defence Systems which it fears could be used by international terrorists to attack civilian aircraft. The report also noted that Cambodia had been accused of being a major source of illegal weapons which armed rebel groups across Asia, including the Tamil Tigers in Sri Lanka and separatists in Indonesia's Aceh province.

Chapter 3: A Maritime Terror Strike — Where and How?

[1] White House, Office of the Press Secretary, remarks by US National Security Advisor Condoleezza Rice to the National Legal Center for the Public Interest, Waldorf Astoria Hotel, New York, 30 October 2003; Speech by US Secretary of Homeland Security Tom Ridge to IDSS, Singapore, op. cit., pp. 2, 4; Fred Kelly, "Anti-Terror Efforts Working, FBI Chief Says", *Indianapolis Star*, 14 November 2003.

The article quotes FBI Director Robert Mueller: "Going into Afghanistan disrupted Al-Qaeda and took away their training grounds".

[2] Speech by Admiral Thomas Fargo, op. cit.; "Jemaah Islamiyah in South East Asia: Damaged but still Dangerous", International Crisis Group Report no. 63, 26 August 2003, pp. 1–2; "Purported New Terror Chief in Indonesia Plotting Attacks", Associated Press, 19 November 2003; Raymond Bonner, "Officials Fear New Attacks by Militants in Southeast Asia", *NYT*, 22 November 2003, Australia's Minister Senator Robert Hill, "Regional Terrorism, Global Security and the Defence of Australia", Speech to the RUSI Triennial International Seminar, Canberra, 9 October 2003; Introductory remarks by Singapore's Minister for Home Affairs Wong Kan Seng to the IDSS Counter-terrorism Forum, 9 March 2004; Speech by Singapore's Minister for Home Affairs, Wong Kan Seng, at the inaugural Asia Pacific Homeland Summit and Exposition in Hawaii, 20 November 2002. Mr Wong said:

> Many of those involved in the Bali bombings of October 2002 have been arrested and prosecuted. The Al-Qaeda's closest ally in South East Asia, the Jemaah Islamiyah, or JI, terrorist organizations has been under pressure from security scrutiny and its regional networks have, in varying degrees, been disrupted. Its key leaders like Hambali have been arrested. Operations have been mounted against elements in the JI network in Cambodia, Thailand, Malaysia, Indonesia, Philippines, Singapore and even Australia.
>
> However, the terrorist threat remains. This is because the JI as an organization is only disrupted. It is by no means eliminated. What is the reason for the JI's resilience? It is because the JI is capable of re-generating itself...both at the leadership as well as the working or operational level. We continue, therefore, not only to live in troubled times but to also expect that such troubled times are going to last for a long time.

[3] Singapore Government, "Jemaah Islamiyah Arrests and the Threat of Terrorism", pp. 3–5; Jemaah Islamiyah in South East Asia, op. cit., pp. 2–10 and 16–23; Alan Sipress and Ellen Nakashima, "Al-Qaeda

Affiliate Training Indonesians on Philippine Island", *Washington Post*, 17 November 2003; Luz Baguioro, "JI Trained Hundreds of Men in Philippine Camp", *Straits Times*, 19 November 2003; "Indonesian Militants Training Philipine Rebels in the South: Official", AFP, 30 November 2003.

⁴ Jessica Stern, "The Protean Enemy: What's Next from Al-Qaeda", *Foreign Affairs*, July/August 2003; Douglas Jehl and Don van Natta Jr., "Analysts See Terrorism Paradox: A Weaker Al-Qaeda Despite Attacks", *NYT*, 21 November 2003.

⁵ Testimony of CIA Director George Tenet on 24 February 2004.

⁶ Douglas Farah and Peter Finn, "Al-Qaeda's Terror Style Spreading". *Washington Post*, 21 November 200; Jemaah Islamiyah in South East Asia, op. cit., pp. 2–10.

⁷ Jemaah Islamiyah in South East Asia, op. cit., "Post 9/11 Terror Attacks Stem from Afghan Training Camps", Associated Press, 23 November 2003.

⁸ Fareed Zakaria, "We Need to Get The Queen Bees", *Newsweek*, 1 December 2003, based on an interview with Singapore's Senior Minister Lee Kuan Yew.

Lee made it clear that the world was facing a foe it could not negotiate with. "Many Europeans think they can finess the problem, that if they don't upset Muslim countries and treat Muslims well, the terrorists won't target them," he said. "But look at Southeast Asia. Muslims have prospered here. But still, Muslim terrorism and militancy have infected them.

Mr Lee was critical of both sides of the Atlantic alliance on Iraq. "When America and Europe are divided, when Japan is hesitant, the extremists are emboldened and think they can win against a divided group. The terrorists' tactics for the time being are to hit only Americans, Jews and America's strong supporters, the British, the Italians, the Turks, warning the Japanese but leaving others alone. They intend to divide and conquer."

⁹ Sebastian Rotella and Richard C. Paddock, "Experts See Major Shift in Al-Qaeda's Strategy", *Los Angeles Times*, 19 February 2003; and "Al-Qaeda: The Whole vs the Parts", *Stratfor Global Intelligence Analysis*, 21 November 2003.

¹⁰ "Turkey Blasts Linked to Asian Terror: Analysts", AFP, 21 November 2003; "Leading Al-Qaeda Expert Says Al-Qaeda Shifting Targets, Strategy", East-West Center Wire, Honolulu, 21 November 2003.

The expert quoted in the East-West Center Wire is Rohan Gunaratna, who warned prophetically in January 2003 that, as Al-Qaeda decentralized still further in response to the US-led crackdown on its former bases of operation, it would rely increasingly on like-minded groups in Southeast Asia, South Asia, the Horn of Africa, the Middle East and the Caucasus to strike at its enemies, mainly Western targets in those areas and operations against Muslim rulers and regimes supporting the US-led war on terror. He said that a wider range of targets would be selected and mass casualty attacks would grow, especially suicide bombings of economic targets and population centres.

Gunaratna also wrote that the "hardening of land aviation targets will shift the threat to maritime targets, particularly to commercial shipping." He added that because of the difficulty of hijacking aircraft to ram them into targets, Al-Qaeda would acquire and use hand-held surface-to-air missiles (SAMs). "If appropriate and immediate countermeasures are not taken to target the Al-Qaeda shipping network", he said, "SAMs under Al-Qaeda control held in the Pakistan-Kashmir-Afghanistan theatre, the Arabian Peninsula, and the Horn of Africa will find its way to East Asia and to Europe, and possibly even to North America." (Rohan Gunaratna, "Al-Qaeda's Trajectory in 2003", IDSS Commentaries, January 2003).

[11] "Terrorists have the Will to Use Dirty Bombs, US Officials Warns", Associated Press, 8 February 2004.

[12] *Economist*, 4 October 2003, "Terrorism and Business: Peril on the Sea".

[13] Aegis Terrorism Report 2003, <www.aegisdef.com>.

[14] International Labour Organisation, Press Release on Women Seafarers, 3 October 2003; Peter Morris, chairman of the International Commission on Shipping to the Apostleship of the Sea XXI World Congress in Rio de Janeiro, 1 October 2002, p. 6.

[15] *Economist*, 13 September 2003, "Flags of Peace?"; Beth Jinks, *Business Times*, (Singapore) [BT], 9 September 2003, "Asian Owners Reject Proposed Wage Hike".

[16] IMO website report on the Maritime Safety Committee at its 74th session in June 2001 receiving the SIRC study; IMO, SIRC's abridged report, <www.imo.org>.

[17] OECD, "Report on Security in Maritime Transport", pp. 13, 14.

[18] Peter Morris, op. cit., pp. 10, 11.

[19] ITF, Flags of Convenience Campaign Update, September 2003 pp. 18 and 19; Testimony to the US House of Representatives' Armed Services Committee Merchant Marine Panel 13 June 2002, by David Cockroft, the ITF's General Secretary.

[20] ILO website, C185 Seafarers' Identity Documents Convention (Revised), 2003, adopted by the ILO's General Conference on 19 June

2003, <www.ilo.org>; Donald Urquhart, "High-tech ID for Seafarers Moves Closer to Reality", *BT*, 12 June 2003.

21 "Biometrics: Too Flaky to Trust", and "Prepare to be Scanned", *Economist*, 6 December 2003; BBC, East Asia Today, 20 June 2003, interview with David Osler, maritime expert and industrial editor of *Lloyd's List*.

22 UNCTAD, "Review of Maritime Transport".

23 US Department of Energy, World Oil Transit Chokepoints; BP, Statistical Review of World Energy.

24 UNCTAD, "Review of Maritime Transport", 2003.

25 "Tanker Industry Seeks Anti-terrorism Measures", *BT*, 3 December 2002. The article quotes Ben Venzke, chief executive of IntelCenter, a security consulting firm in Alexandria, Virginia, "To hit a tanker with a boat full of explosives is not much more difficult than getting into your car and driving into a fuel truck on the interestate. "The vulnerability of tankers and other petroleum facilities has always been there. It's just that Al-Qaeda is now choosing to exploit that vulnerability."

26 BP, Statistical Review of World Energy; World Oil Transit Chokepoints; Energy Security Initiative: Emergency Oil Stocks as an Option to Respond to Oil Supply Disruptions, a background report in 2002 by the Asia Pacific Energy Research Centre; Sam Bateman, Sealane Security, paper presented on 8 September 2003 to the APEC High-level Conference on Maritime Security, Manila.

27 Robert C. Beckman, Enhancing Maritime Security in the Straits of Malacca and Singapore, Paper presented to the Conference of the Institute for Ocean Policy, Ship & Ocean Foundation, Tokyo, 17–18 October 2003; Danny Chan, Modern Maritime Threats and Strategies, op. cit.

28 Donald Urquhart, "Tankers Prime Terrorist Target in Strait: Seminar", *BT*, 30 April 2002.

29 Sam Bateman, Sealane Security; Ambassador Makarim Wibison, Chairman of the APEC Counter Terrorism Task Force, speech given at APEC High-level Conference on Maritime Security, Manila, 8 September 2003; World Oil Transit Chokepoints; op. cit.; Mansoor Ijaz, "The Maritime Threat from Al-Qaeda", *Financial Times*, 20 October 2003; "Modern Maritime Threats and Strategies", *Financial Times*, 13 October 2003; "China Fuels Rise in Shipping Rates", *ASWJ*, 5 November 2003; "High Shipping Costs to Affect Consumers"; *Financial Times*, 25 November 2003; "China's Rapid Expansion Boosts World Shipping Industry", *Economist Pocket World in Figures 2003*, p. 32.

[30] World Oil Transit Chokepoints.

[31] Reuters, 20 November: "The logical thing to do is to see an increased threat", said Kevin O'Brien, a policy analyst with RAND Europe. "In real chokepoints like the Bosphorus and Suez Canal, you can make an attack with a small vessel or even a shore-mounted missile, as we've seen in the Persian Gulf. You don't need a lot of ground to launch one of these things".

But maritime security consultant Les Chapman of Control Risks Group in London said that the attacks on Turkey had been on high profile targets — synagogues, international business and the British government — and that there was no reason why strikes should be directed at shipping. "Suicide bombing on a ship is very difficult", he said. "We can see no sign at all from the Islamic extremists to say there is any specific threat in the Bosphorus or eastern Mediterranean".

[32] UNCTAD, "Annual Review of Maritime Transport", p. 41; "The Prestige Oil Spill: A Game of Consequences", *Economist*, 23 November 2002; Paul Geitner, "New Oil Spill from Old Tanker Prompts Renewed Calls for Crackdown on Environmental Timebombs," Associated Press, 21 November 2002; Bhushan Bahree, Carlta Vitzthum and Erik Portanger, "Tanker Saga Illustrates how Rescues are Hurt by Cross-current Goals", *ASWJ*, 25 November 2002.

[33] International Association of Independent Tanker Owners (Intertanko), Intertanko Welcomes International Accord at IMO on Amendents to MARPOL, <www.intertanko.com>, December 2003; Amended European Regulation on Single Hull Tankers took Effect 21 October 2003", <www.intertanko.com>; Beth Jinks, "Tanker in Row Clears Spain's Coast", *BT*, 17 December 2003; "Asian Nations Consider Joint Stockpiles", *Straits Times*, 6 December 2003; "China Changing World Oil-demand Map", China Daily website, 14 November 2003.

[34] Beth Jinks, "Ships Collide in S'pore Waters; Oil Spill Contained", *BT*, 6 December 2003.

[35] Associated Press report in *Portsmouth Herald*, 11 October 2001, "Report Says Risks of LNG Explosion in Boston Slight; "Energy Security and Liquified Natural Gas", *Global Energy Security Analysis*, 26 September 2003.

[36] OECD, "Report on Safety, Security in Maritime Transport", p. 17.

[37] Platts, What is LNG?, <www.platts.com>; Weaver's Cove Energy, "Safety", <www/weaverscore/com/Safety2.html>; ChevronTexaco Corp presentation by Doug Quillen to Natural Gas Technology conference in Houston, Texas, 14–15 May 2002, "LNG Safety: Myths and Legends"; Tux Turkel, "Vigilance Attends LNG Deliveries", *Portland Press Herald*, 6 October 2003.

38 US Department of Energy Report February 2002; California Energy Commission, Staff White Paper on Liquified Natural Gas in California: History, Risks and Siting, July 2003; Jerry Havens, "Terrorism: Ready to Blow?" *Bulletin of the Atomic Scientists* 59, July/August 2003, pp. 16–18; "LNG Attack may Devastate Boston Port", *BT*, 11 November 2003.

39 "Report on Security in Maritime Transport", pp. 10, 11; "Police ID Explosives from Turkish Attacks", Associated Press, 28 November 2003; "Bombs in Istanbul Attacks Bear Al-Qaeda Stamp."

40 Robert Go, "Jakarta Seeks Tight Watch on Explosives", *Straits Times*, 25 September 2003; BBC Worldwide Monitoring, 20 September 2003, "Indonesia Admits Difficulty Controlling Explosives Production".

41 Associated Press, 24 June 2003, "Greeks Probe Terror Link to Cargo Ship"; ITF press statement and factfile on Baltic Sky intercepted carrying explosives, 23 June 2003; Reuters, 24 June 2003, "NATO Hunting 20 Suspect Ships"; BBC news, 26 June 2003, "New Explosives Cargo Mystery"; "NATO Terror Tipoff on Explosives Ship Sailing to Sudan", *Guardian*, 24 June 2003,.

42 CNN, "Texas Town Recalls Horror of Nation's Worst Industrial Accident", 16 April 1997; Steve Olafson, "Texas City Just Blew Up", *Houston Chronicle*, 16 April 1997; The Handbook of Texas Online: Texas City Disaster, <www.tsha.utexas.edu/handbook/online/articles/view/TT/lyt1>.

Chapter 4: Mega-Terror — Radiological and Nuclear

[1] Maritime Advisory (MARAD) issued on 23 October 2002 by the US Government's National Infrastructure Protection Centre to operators of US flag and effective US-controlled vessels and other maritime interests.

The advisory to ship operators noted that an audio message from Osama bin Laden, taped on an undetermined date and broadcast by Al Jazeera on 6 October 2002, refers to Al-Qaeda targeting key sectors of the US economy. Bin Laden's chief deputy, Ayman al-Zawahri, reiterated the threat in the closing line of an audio taped interview released on 9 October 2002.

The advisory went on:

> The focus on economic targets is consistent with Al-Qaeda's stated ideological goals and longstanding strategy. The September 11 (2001) attacks (on the US) and commentary on these attacks by bin Laden and others indicate how central economic targets are to this strategy: the group's leaders have said that they aim to undermine what they see as the backbone of US power, the economy. Our adversary is trying to portray American influence as based on economic might and therefore seeks to strike an economic target prominent enough for economic and symbolic reasons that it would have immediate resonance around the world.
>
> Recipients should review and implement additional prudent steps to detect, disrupt, deter and defend against potential attacks against our nation's critical transportation infrastructure and installations at home and abroad.

[3] John Zarocostas, "Energy Security New Top Priority", *Straits Times*, 29 November 2003,.

The report quoted Admiral Thomas Collins, commandant of the US Coast Guard, as telling a Senate panel: "A terrorist incident against our maritime transportation system would have a devastating and long-lasting impact on global shipping, international trade and the world economy."

[4] "Tanker Industry Seeks Anti-terrorism Measures", *BT*, 3 December 2002.

[5] Tech Central Station website, 11 November 2003, "The Political Economy of Terror", by Ariel Cohen, a Research Fellow at The Heritage Foundation in Washington whose expertise includes international energy security. He writes: "Bin Laden and his henchmen understand well the political economy of terror. They aim for maximum ripple effect...", <www.techcentralstation.com>.

6 Tony Santiago, "Political Risk could Cost World Economy $1 Trillion", *EeTimes*, 6 February 2004.

7 Testimony of George J. Tenet, pp. 3, 4; Terrorist CBRN: Materials and Effects, posted CIA website June 2003; "Terrorists have the Will to use Dirty Bombs, US Officials Warns", Associated Press, 8 February 2004; CBS News, 24 April 2002, "The Fear of Radiation".

8 Terrorism: Q&A on Dirty Bombs posted on the website of the US Council on Foreign Relations in cooperation with the Markle Foundation; ABC News, 17 September 2003, "What is a Dirty Bomb?"; Testimony on dirty bombs by Dr Henry Kelly, President of the Federation of American Scientists to the Senate Committee on Foreign Relations, 6 March 2003; International Atomic Energy Agency (IAEA) press release, 1 November 2002, "Calculating the New Global Nuclear Terrorism Threat".

9 IAEA report in 2003, Inadequate Control of World's Radioactive Sources, Statement on 11 March 2003 by IAEA Director General Dr Mohamed ElBaradei to the International Conference on Security of Radioactive Sources; Testimony on dirty bombs by Dr Henry Kelly; Joby Warrick, "Smugglers Targeting Dirty Bombs for Profit: Radioactive Materials are Sought Worldwide", *Washington Post*, 30 November 2003; Bennett Ramberg, "Terrorism has Altered the Nuclear Equation Forever", *IHT*, 10 December 2003; James Jay Carafano and Jack Spencer, "Dealing with Dirty Bombs: Plain Facts, Practical Solutions", The Heritage Foundation, background paper no. 1723, 27 January 2004.

10 Joby Warrick, "Dirty Bomb Fears Spur a Hunt for Soviet Relics", *IHT*, 12 November 2002; Shawn W Crispin and Gary Fields, "Seizure Triggers Dirty Bomb Fear", *AWSJ*, 18 June 2003; "Dirty Bomb Materials in Africa Heighten Terror Concern", *Financial Times*, 18 June 2003; James Hookway, "Did Thai Teacher Want to Help Make Bombs, or Just a Quick Profit?", *AWSJ*, 1 August 2003; "US Dirty Bomb Danger Real", CBS News, 10 November 2003; Joby Warrick, "Dirty Bomb Rockets Vanish: Arms Made in Caucasus Feared Sold to Terrorists", *Washington Post*, 7 December 2003.

11 Frank Gardner, "Al-Qaeda was Making Dirty Bomb", BBC, 31 January 2003; Joby Warrick, "Smugglers Targeting Dirty Bombs for Profit: Radioactive Materials are Sought Worldwide", *Washington Post*, 30 November 2003.

12 "Dirty Bomb Materials in Africa Heighten Terror Concern"; "Smugglers Targeting Dirty Bombs for Profit"; James and Glanz and Andrew C. Revkin, "Materials at Hand for a Dirty Bomb"; Terrorist CBRN: Materials and Effects.

[13] Joby Warrick, "Study Raises Project for 'Dirty Bomb' Toll", *Washington Post*, 13 January 2004.

[14] Official US Department of Justice transcript, 10 June 2002, of the statement by US Attorney General John Ashcroft regarding the transfer of Abdullah Al Muhajir (born Jose Padilla) to the Department of Defense as an enemy combatant.

[15] US Government response on 28 August 2002 to, and motion to dismiss, an amended petition for a writ of habeas corpus for Jose Padilla, in the US District Court for the southern district of New York; Official transcript of press conference on 10 June 2002 by Deputy US Defense Secretary Paul Wolfowitz and FBI Director Robert Mueller; ABC news, 10 June 2002, "Officials: Dirty Bomb Plot Disrupted"; CNN, 28 August 2002, "Prosecutors: Suspect did 'Dirty Bomb' Research in Pakistan."

[16] The White House order to the Secretary of Defense, signed 9 June 2002 by the US President; CNN, 17 November 2003, Phil Hirschkorn and Deborah Feyerick, "Dirty Bomb Suspect Appeals Detention", "US to Seek Stay of Court Ruling on Padilla", Reuters, 18 December 2003.

[17] Charles Lane, "Court Accepts Case of 'Dirty Bomb' Suspect", *Washington Post*, 21 February 2004; Michael Powell, "Lawyer Visits 'Dirty Bomb' Suspect", *Washington Post*, 4 March 2004.

[18] Deputy US Defence Secretary Paul Wolfowitz and FBI Director Robert Mueller, Official transcript of press conference, 10 June 2002; CBS, 16 June 2002; Tony Karon, "Report: Padilla was Told to Lower Sights"; "The Dirty Bomb Suspect: Lots of Questions, Few Answers", *Time*, 11 June 2002.

[19] Hugh Bronstein, "British Man Faces Dirty Bomb Charge in US," Reuters, 19 December 2003; BBC news, 19 December 2003, "Briton Faces Dirty Bomb Charge".

[20] "Terror Attack is Worst Nightmare for US Ports", *BT*, 12 December 2003.

[21] Press release by US Department of Energy, 13 August 2003, US and Dutch Governments Launch Effort to Detect Terrorist Shipments of Nuclear Material.

[22] US Council on Foreign Relations in cooperation with the Markle Foundation, Q&A on Terrorism and Making a Nuclear Bomb; Peter Grier, "Loose Nukes", *Christian Science Monitor*, 5 December 2001; CNN, 17 November 2001, "Al-Qaeda Documents, Manuals found in Kabul: Papers Reveal Plans to Construct Nuclear Weapons"; Jamie McIntyre, "Zubaydah: Al-Qaeda had 'Dirty Bomb' Know-how", CNN, 22 April 2002; Testimony of George J. Tenet, pp. 3–4; Terrorist CBRN: Materials and Effects, op. cit.

[23] Graham Allison, "How to Stop Nuclear Terror", *Foreign Affairs*, January/February 2004, pp. 1–2; Frank Barnaby, "How to Build a Nuclear Bomb and Other Weapons of Mass Destruction (London, New York: Granta Books, 2003), pp. 70–83; Dana Priest, "US Boosts Musharraf Security", *Washington Post* report in the *AWSJ*, 5 January 2004; Victoria Burnett, "Concerns over Pakistan's Deadly Nuclear Know-how Brings a Stream of Western Visitors to its Door", *Financial Times*, 6 March 2004; Mansoor Ijaz and R. James Woolsey, "How Secure is Pakistan's Plutonium", *NYT*, 28 November 2001; IAEA press release, 1 November 2002, Calculating the New Global Nuclear Terrorism Threat.

[24] Calculating the New Global Nuclear Terrorism Threat; Steven Erlanger, "Loose Nukes"; Q&A on Terrorism and Making a Nuclear Bomb, op. cit.; Terrorist CBRN, op. cit.

[25] Todd S. Purdum, "Security Proves a Long, Hard Endeavor", *NYT* report in *IHT*, 10 September 2002; Michael Levi, "Nuclear Dangers Beyond Iraq", *NYT*, 23 September 2002,

[26] Interparliamentary Conference Edition and Supplement: Pledge Analysis, <www.sgpproject.org>, Global Partnership Update, no. 2, November 2003; Matthew Bunn, Preventing Nuclear Terrorism: A Progress Update, report co-sponsored by the Nuclear Threat Initiative and the Project on Managing the Atom in the Belfer Center for Science and International Affairs, John F. Kennedy School of Government, Harvard University, 22 October 2003, pp. 2–5; "West Faulted for Poor WMD Security", Reuters, 18 November 2003; Nikola Krastev, "US Sees Dollars in Russian Nuclear Technology", Radio Free Europe, report in *Asia Times*, 12 December 2002.

[27] Q&A on Terrorism and Making a Nuclear Bomb, op. cit.

[28] "Security Proves a Long, Hard Endeavor".

[29] "Experts Worry Terrorists have Nuke Plans", Associated Press, 4 February 2004; Anton La Guardia, Ahmed Rashid and Alec Russell, "The Nuclear Supermarket", Daily Telegraph online, 6 February 2004; President George Bush, text of speech on 11 February 2004, the National Defence University, Washington, D.C., on new measures to counter the threat of weapons of mass destruction; Council on Foreign Relations, Q&A: Black Market Nuclear Proliferation, 12 February 2004; William J. Broad, David E. Sanger and Raymond Bonner, "A Tale of Nuclear Proliferation: How Pakistani Built His Network", *NYT*, 12 February 2004; Joby Warrick and Peter Slevi, "Arms Plans are Traced to China", *Washington Post*, 15 February 2004; Bernard-Henri Levy, "The Story Doesn't End with Khan", *AWSJ*, 18 February 2004; Murray Hiebert, "Spreading Fear", *Far Eastern Economic Review*,

19 February 2004; Jonathan Ansfield, "China Nuke Plans Surface in Libya", Reuters, 17 February 2004; Craig S. Smith, "Roots of Pakistan Atomic Scandal Traced to Europe", *NYT*, 19 February 2004; Peter Slevin, "Libya Made Plutonium, Nuclear Watchdog Says".

30 Avalon Project, Damages Caused by Atomic Bombs, Yale Law School; Father P. Siemes, The Atomic Bombing of Hiroshima, an Eyewitness Account, <www.yale.edu/lawweb/avalon/abomb/>; Matthew Bunn, Preventing Nuclear Terrorism, pp. 3–4.

31 Voice of America, 9 February 2004, "18 Years after Chernobyl Disaster, Millions Still Suffer".

Chapter 5: Castrophic Terrorism and its Potential Impact on Global Trade

1. Speech by former US Senator Sam Nunn, Co-Chairman of the Nuclear Threat Initiative, 16 December 2003, "Kazakhstan: Reducing Nuclear Dangers, Increasing Global Security", p. 4; Frits Bolkestein, op. cit.
2. OECD, Report on Security in Maritime Transport, pp. 17–18; DFAT, Economic Analytical Unit, Global Issues Brief on the Economic Costs of Terrorism, 7 April 2003.
3. Donald Bowserbox and David Closs, "Supply Chain Sustainability and Cost in the New War Economy", *Traffic World*, 1 April 2002; "The Friction Economy", *Fortune*, 3 February 2003.
4. Speech by Jack Short, 21 March 2003, op. cit.
5. Conference Board and Booz Allen Hamilton, Port Security War Game, October 2002.
6. OECD, "Report on Security in Maritime Transport", p. 17.
7. "US Marine Insurers Respond to post-9/11 World of Domestic Security Rules and Regulations", *Insurance Journal of the US*, 3 November 2003; "The Ocean Marine Market: A Unique Animal", *Insurance Journal of the US*, 20 February 2002; UNCTAD, "Review of Maritime Transport", p. 61; Donald Urquhart, "Insurers may Class Indon Piracy Attacks as Terrorism", *BT*, 28 November 2003,
8. Donald Urquhart, "APL Diverting Some Calls from PSA's Aden Terminal", *BT*, 1 November 2002; Beth Jinks, "War Risk Premiums Cut for Ships Calling at Yemen", *BT*, 18 September 2000; Beth Jinks, "PSA Drops Out of Aden Terminal Venture: Report", *BT*, 27 October 2003.
9. Donald Urquhart, "Underwriters Declare Indonesia a War-risk Zone", *BT*, 18 October 2002; Beth Jinks, "All Indon Ports Put Under Marine Insurance Exclusion Zone", *BT*, 26 October 2002.
10. DFAT, Global Issues Brief on the Economic Costs of Terrorism, op. cit.

Chapter 6: Costs and Benefits of Enhanced Security

[1] Robert Bonner, Testimony, <www.imo.org>, op. cit.

[2] IMO website, "IMO Adopts Comprehensive Maritime Security Measures", 9–13 December 2002; Jack Short, op. cit., p. 6; International Shipping Federation website, key issues, "Maritime Security" and "Automatic Identification Systems", <www.marisec.org>.

[3] US Department of Homeland Security, "CSI in brief"; Robert Bonner, Speech, op. cit.

[4] US Department of Homeland Security, "Frequently Asked Questions about CSI", <www.dhs.gov.dhspublic/index.jsp>.

[5] Department of Homeland Security website, "Secretary Ridge announces Container Security Initiative's Phase II", 12 June 2003; Department of Homeland Security website, "China signs declaration of principles with Container Security Initiative to target and pre-screen cargo destined for the US", 18 September 2003, US Department of Transportation, press release, Transportation Secretary Mineta Signs Far-reaching Maritime Agreement with China, 8 December 2003; Philip Shenon, "US to Put Inspectors in Muslim Cargo Ports", *IHT*, 13 June 2003.

[6] "CSI in Brief"; Robert Bonner, op. cit.

[7] Frits Bolkestein, op. cit.

[8] European Community, Customs Authority statement on agreement initialled with the US on transport security cooperation, 18 November 2003; Statement by US Mission to the EC, 18 November 2003; Joint statement of the US Customs and Border Protection and the European Commission, 25 June 2003; Frits Bolkestein, op. cit., EC factsheet on container security; *BT*, 29 January 2003.

[9] Arabinda Acharya, "APEC Summit: Regionalising the War on Terror", *Commentary* 38, 3 November 2003; Alan Oxley, "Trade and Terrorism", Tech Central Station website, 4 November 2003; White House fact sheet, "New APEC Initiatives on Counterterrorism, 21 October 2003; Australian Prime Minister's Office, "Australian APEC Counterterrorism Initiatives", press release, 21 October 2003; APEC Secretariat, information document on Counter Terrorism Action Plan submitted to APEC senior officials meeting in Bangkok, 14–15 October 2003; Speech by Ambassador Makarim Wibisono, op. cit.

[10] K.C. Vijayan and Nicholas Fang, "Satellite-based Ship Tracking System Soon", *Straits Times*, 22 January 2003; OECD, Security in Maritime Transport, pp. 2, 3; Reuters, 17 November 2003, Peter Starck, "US Anti-terror Measure to Raise Shipping Costs", Reuters, 17 November 2003, "Terror Attack is Worst Nightmare for US Ports", *BT*, 12 December 2003.

[11] Leslie Miller, "US Ports, Ships Miss Security Deadline", *Atlanta Journal-Constitution*, 31 December 2003; "Industry Slow to Face up to Potential Attacks", *BT*, Reuters, "Caribbean States Struggling to Meet New Port Security Laws", *BT*, 16 December 2003; Jack Short, op. cit.; Frits Bolkestein, op. cit.; Beth Jinks, "US Govt Urged to Review Funding of Security Measures", *BT*, 25 July 2003; Donald Urquhart, "Studies Undertaken to Probe Supply Chain Security", *BT*, 5 August 2003.

[12] World Shipping Council submission on Operation Safe Commerce to the Transportation Security Administration of the US Department of Transportation, 5 December 2002; Linda Ensor, "US Gets its Way on Cargo Security", <www.allAfrica.com>, 8 December 2003.

[13] European Commission Proposal to the European Parliament on Enhancing Maritime Transport Security, 2 May 2003, p. 14.

[14] Safe InterModal Transport Across the Globe (SIMTAG), progress update, Brussels, 12 May 2003; Secure Trade in the APEC Region: The Bangkok/Laem Chabang Efficient and Secure Trade Project, October 2003; Presentation on Smart and Secure Tradelanes by Gary Gilbert, Chief Security Officer, Hutchison Port Holdings, Hong Kong, to the APEC High-level Meeting on Maritime Security Cooperation, Manila, 8–9 September, 2003; Judi Hasson, "Securing the Homeland: One Container at a Time," *Federal Computer Week*, 8 September 2003; Dan Verton, "Former CIA Chief sees Need for Greater Network Resilience, Market Incentives", *Computerworld*, 29 October 2003.

Chapter 7: How Secure?

1 Tom Ridge, op. cit.; Margaret Wrightson, Director, Homeland Security and Justice Issues, Maritime Security: Progress Made in Implementing Maritime Transportation Security Act, but Concerns Remain, statement before the US Senate Committee on Commerce, Science and Transportation, 9 September 2003; Chloe Albanesius, "Homeland Security Officials Accused of Foot Dragging of Foot Dragging on Port Security, <www.GovExec.com>, 18 December 2003.

2 ABC news, 10 September 2003, "Border Breach? Customs Fails to Detect Depleted Uranium — Again"; ABC news, 11 September 2003, "How Safe are our Borders?"; "Howard Kurtz, "ABC Ships Uranium Overseas for Story", *Washington Post*, 11 September 2003; "Bush Feels the Heat of Maritime Security Worries", *Lloyd's List*, 18 September 2003; Natural Resources Defense Council website, "The ABC News Nuclear Smuggling Experiment: the Sequel".

3 OECD, "Report on Ownership and Control of Ships", March 2003.

4 John Mintz, "15 Freighters Believed to be Linked to Al-Qaeda", *Washington Post*, 31 December 2002; Donald Urquhart, "Mongolia Sets up Shipping Register", *BT*, 12 March 2003; Marc Lifsher, "Bolivia Flag of Convenience Proves all too Convenient for Raft of Dodgy Shippers", *AWSJ*, 24 October 2002; ITF, Flags of Convenience Campaign Update, September 2003.

5 ITF, Flags of Convenience Campaign Update 2003; EU, Overview of Maritime Transport Policy, <www.europa.eu.int/index>; The Japanese Shipowners' Association, Report on the Current State of Japanese Shipping, March 2003.

6 OECD, "Ownership and Control of Ships".

7 Jack Short, op. cit. p. 7.

8 David Cockroft, General Secretary of ITF, Testimony to the US House of Representatives' Armed Services Committee Merchant Marine Panel, 13 June 2002.

9 Paper on Maritime Security: Information on "Ownership" and "Control" of Ships, submitted by the US to the IMO, 26 March 2002.

10 Flag State Audit 2003, Seafarers International Research Centre (SIRC), Cardiff University.

11 Flags of Convenience Campaign Update 2003; ITF, Flags of Convenience Campaign Report 2001/02, July 2002.

12 Marcus Hand, "Cambodia to Take Back Control of Ship Registry", *Lloyd's List*, 26 August 2002; Beth Jinks, "ITF Slams Cambodia's Decision on Ship Registry", *BT*, 14 January 2003; "Cambodia Launches Probe after Cambodian-flagged Ship Seized off Africa", AFP, 14 June 2003.

[13] Associated Press, 14 June 2002, "French Commandos Seize Cocaine Ship"; AFP, 14 June 2002, "Greek Officials Arrest Owners of Cambodia-flagged Ship after Drug Bust"; "Cambodian PM gave Permission to Raid Ship in Drug Bust: Minister", AFP, 17 June 2002.

[14] Elaine Keogh, "Million-pound Cigarette Haul Seized from Ship", *Irish Times*, 8 November 2001; Baltic News Service, 9 November 2001, "Smuggling Haul from Estonia Linked to Irish Dissident Republicans"; Baltic News Service, 15 November 2001, "IRA Contraband Belongs to 20-year-old Estonian".

[15] Flag State Audit 2003, Report on Cambodia, op. cit.; Beth Jinks, "ITF Slams Cambodia's Decision on Ship Registry".

[16] Michael Richardson, "Terrorism Roams the High Seas under Flags of Convenience", *Straits Times*, 22 May 2003; Michael Richardson, "Raid at Sea Highlights Flag Abuses", *IHT*, 24 June 2002.

[17] "ITF Slams Cambodia's Decision on Ship Registry"; "Winner Registry is the Loser as Cambodia Acts", *Lloyds List*, 24 June 2002; Paris Memorandum on Port State Control, <www.parismou.org>.

[18] "Cambodia to Take Back Control of Ship Registry"; "ITF slams Cambodia's Decision on Ship Registry"; ITF media release, 10 January 2003.

[19] "Tonga Pulls Plug on Troubled Flag", *Lloyds List*, 20 May 2002; "The Ships that Died of Shame"; *Sydney Morning Herald*, 14 January 2003; "Island Nation of Tonga Linked to the Al-Qaeda", AFP, 3 January 2003; John Mintz, "15 Freighters Believed to be Linked to Al-Qaeda", *BT*, 20 May 2002; Donald Urquhart, "Tonga Closing Down International Ship Registry", *BT*, 20 May 2002. ITF news on-line, 21 March 2002, "Italy 'Refugee Ship' Used Flags of Convenience for 15 Years; Luke Baker, "Italy Study Sees Al-Qaeda Link to Human Trafficking", Reuters, 7 September 2003; ITF, Flags of Convenience Campaign Update, September 2003.

Chapter 8: Proliferation Security Initiative

1 White House text of Remarks by the President to the People of Poland, 31 May 2003; Proliferation Security Initiative: Statement of Interdiction Principles, fact sheet issued by the US State Department, 3 September 2003; International Institute of Strategic Studies, London, *Strategic Comment* 9, no. 6, August 2003.

2 Address by the Secretary of Australia's Department of Foreign Affairs and Trade, Dr Ashton Calvert, to the Royal United Services Institute (RUSI) International Seminar on Global Security in the New Millennium Canberra, 9–10 October 2003; Interview with John Bolton, US Undersecretary of State for Arms Control and International Security, US State Department, 4 December 2003.

3 Arms Control Association, fact sheet: The Nuclear Nonproliferation Treaty at a glance, May 2003; Interview with John Bolton, op. cit., John Bolton, Testimony to the US House of Representatives International Relations Committee, 4 June 2003; K. Subrahmanyam, "US Security Initiative: An Invitation India Cannot Turn Down", *Times of India*, 13 October 2003.

4 "Bush Targets Drug Trade Linked to North Korea", Associated Press report in the *IHT*, 17 September 2003; Paul E. Simons, Acting US Assistant Secretary of State for International Narcotics and Law Enforcement, Testimony on narcotics source countries, to the House of Representatives Committee on Government Reform, 9 July 2003; *NYT* report in the *IHT*, 23 August 2003; James Brooke, "Huge North Korea Aid Holds Hope and Peril"; Jay Solomon and Haw Won Choi, "Shadowy Business Arm Helps Regime Keep Grip on Power in Pyongyang", *AWSJ*, 14 July 2003; Jay Solomon and Jason Dean, "North Korea Tied to the Drug Trade", *AWSJ*, 23 April 2003; *NYT* report in the *IHT*, 22 May 2003, James Dao, "Pyongyang Said to be Profiting from Drugs"; Anthony Spaeth, "Kim's Rackets", *Time*, 9 June 2003; *Financial Times*, 5 June 2003, Andrew Ward, "N Korea Suspected Source of Drugs Seized in South", *The Age*, 24 May 2003, Shane Geen, "Dear Leader Implicated in Japanese Drugs Trial", *AWSJ*, 6 February 2003; Bertil Lintner and Steve Stecklow, "North Korea's Missile Maze", YaleGlobal online, 5 May 2003, Bertil Lintner, "North Korea's Missile Trade Helps Fund its Nuclear Program", *Washington Post*, 14 August 2003, Joby Warrick, "On North Korean Freighter, a Hidden Missile Factory"; CIA, report to the US Congress on weapons proliferation trends during the first half of 2003, 10 November 2003.

5 Official transcript of speech by John Bolton, US Undersecretary of State for Arms Control and International Security, at the opening of a conference on security issues, Institute of Foreign Policy Analysis and

the Fletcher School of Tufts University, Washington, 2 December 2003; John Larkin and Donald Macintyre, "Arsenal of the Axis — North Korea Already Supplies Missiles to Rogue States; Now it Poses a New Threat: Nuclear Proliferation", *Time*, 14 July 2003; Ivo H. Daalder and James M. Lindsay, "Nuclear Wal-Mart?" *American Prospect* 14, no. 8, 1 September 2003.

[6] Official transcript of media interview by Australia's Defence Minister Senator Robert Hill on the PSI Coral Sea exercise, 13 September 2003; Interview with John Bolton, op. cit.

[7] Official transcript of answers to questions by Australia's Foreign Minister Alexander Downer after his address to the National Press Club, Canberra, 26 November 2003; U.S. State Department Transcript of Interview with John Bolton, by the Arms Control Association, 4 December 2003; IMO summary of legal committee session, 28 April–2 May 2003; Presentation by Robert Beckman, Faculty of Law, National University of Singapore, to the CSCAP/PECC Joint Meeting on Maritime Security in Manila, 6–7 September 2003.

[8] Edward Harris, "Pact Gives US Search Rights Over Ships", Associated Press, 13 February 2004; Transcript of US State Department spokesman Richard Boucher, 13 February 2004, pp. 8, 9; Board-and-search WMD Initiative Strengthened by Deal with Liberia, <www.CNSNews.com>, 13 February 2004.

[9] Reuters, 25 February 2004, "UK Wants to Search Ships for WMD"; Press Association report, "Straw Outlines WMD Crackdown Plans", *Scotsman*, 25 February 2004.

[10] Joby Warrick, "N. Korea Shops Stealthily for Nuclear Arms Gear: Front Companies Step up Efforts in European Market", *Washington Post*, 15 August 2003.

[11] International Institute of Strategic Studies, *Strategic Comment* 9, no. 6, August 2003.

[12] "Asia-Pacific Powers to Cooperate in Blocking WMD-related Exports to N Korea", AFP, 27 October 2993; "Nations Target Illegal Exports to North Korea", *Japan Times*, 28 October 2003.

[13] Shane Green, "Pyongyang to Face New Restrictions on Trade", *The Age*, 28 October 2003.

[14] "Asia-Pacific Powers to Cooperate in Blocking WMD-related Exports to N Korea", AFP, 27 October 2003; "Nations Target Illegal Exports to North Korea", *Japan Times*, 28 October 2003.

[15] "Japan to Tighten Export Rules on Potential Weapons", Reuters, 9 December 2003.

[16] Christopher Cooper, "Taiwan Seizes North Korean Cargo", *AWSJ*, 13 August 2003; "US Praises Taiwan for Intercepting Chemical Weapons

Precursor from North Korea", AFP, 13 August 2003; Robert Marquand, "Ship's Seizure Sends Warning to N. Korea", *Christian Science Monitor*, 12 August 2003.

[17] Speech by US President George Bush on WMD proliferation to the National Defence University in Washington, 11 February 2004, pp. 2–4; Testimony by George J. Tenet, p. 8; William J. Broad, David E. Sanger and Raymond Bonner, "A Tale of Nuclear Proliferation: How Pakistani Built His Network", *NYT*, 12 February 2004.

[18] Transcript of Interview with John Bolton, op. cit., n.7.

[19] Andrew Ward, "North Korea Seeks Incentives Before Talks", *Financial Times*, 10 December 2003,

[20] English text of the official White Paper on China's Non-Proliferation Policy and Measures, *China Daily*, 4 December 2003; Associated Press report in the *NYT*, 3 December 2003, "China Outlines Nonproliferation Plans"; BBC, 3 December 2003, "China Explains WMD Policy."

[21] "FM Stresses Nation's Proliferation Stance", China Daily, 5 December 2003.

[22] Voice of America, 3 December 2003, "US welcomes China's commitment to wmd non-proliferation"; official transcript of speech by US Secretary of State Colin Powell on 5 November 2003 at the Conference on China-US Relations, George Bush School of Government and Public Service, Texas A & M University; Bill Gertz, "N Korea Using China to Obtain Missile Supplies", *Washington Times*, 22 January 2003.

[23] Guy Dinmore and Andrew Ward, "US Seeks Help from China and Russia to Curb the Spread of WMD", *Financial Times*, 10 September 2003; "China and North Korea — Preparing for the Worst", *Economist*, 20 September 2003; *NYT* report in the *IHT*, 16 September 2003; Joseph Kahn, "China Puts Troops on its Border with Korea", *Straits Times*, 15 September 2003, "China Sends 150,000 troops to N Korean Border".

[24] "Australia Seizes Vessel Owned by North Korea", *AWSJ*, 22 April 2003; Anna Fifield and Andrew Ward, "Australia Seizes More Heroin", *Financial Times*, 28 May 2003; Official transcript of press conference in Adelaide by Australian Foreign Minister Alexander Downer, 2 May 2003; "Australia Warns North Korea over Drug Smuggling", Reuters, 2 May 2003; Official transcript of press conference in Tokyo by Australian Foreign Minister Alexander Downer, 15 May 2003; Jay Solomon, "Pyongyang Denies Ties to Heroin-drug Trade", *AWSJ*, 7 May 2003; Steven R. Weisman, "US-led Naval Exercise is Signal to North Korea", *IHT*, 18 August 2003.

[25] Carla Anne Robbins, "Why US Sidestepped UN in its Plan to Halt Shipments of Weapons", *AWSJ*, 23 October 2003; Official transcript of remarks by US Defence Secretary Donal Rumsfeld at an American Chamber of Commerce joint breakfast meeting in Seoul on 18 November 2003; Brian Knowlton, "North Korean Ship Seized with Scuds", *IHT*, 12 December 2002; Greg Jaffe, Carla Anne Robbins and Charles Hutzler, "Scud Find Gives US New Impetus", *AWSJ*, 12 December 2002; "What Have We Here?", *Economist*, 14 December 2002; Carla Anne Robbins, David S. Cloud and Yaroslav Trofimov, "US Miscalculated in Scud Affair", *AWSJ*, 13 December 2002; Bill Gertz, "Ship Gets Arms in and out", *Washington Times*, 18 February 2003.

Chapter 9: Sea Change and Recommendations

1 David Hughes, "IMO has to Deal with Conflicting Winds of Change", *BT*, 3 December 2003; Toby Shelley, "Guidelines Set on Use of Flags of Convenience", *Financial Times*, 26 November 2003,

2 IMO <www.imo.org>; International Transport Workers' Federation, Flags of Convenience Campaign Update, September 2003.

3 UNCTAD, "Review of Maritime Transport", 2002.

4 ITF, Flags of Convenience Campaign Update; Japanese Shipowners' Association, Report on the Current State of Japanese Shipping, March 2003; George Joseph, "S'pore Vows to Maintain Quality Merchant Fleet", *BT*, 23 July 2002.

5 Beth Jinks, "Tax Perks Draw World's Top Shipping Group", *BT*, 4 March 2004.

6 UNCTAD, Review of Maritime Transport, pp. 36, 37.

7 Toby Shelley, "Guidelines Set on Use of Flags of Convenience", *Financial Times*, 26 November 2003; David Hughes, "IMO Has to Deal with Conflicting Winds of Change", *BT*, 3 December 2003.

8 ITF media release, "ITF tells Congress Flags of Convenience Endanger USA", 13 June 2002.

References

Allison, Graham. "How to Stop Nuclear Terror", *Foreign Affairs*, January/February, 2004.

Asia Pacific Energy Research Centre. Energy Security Initiative: Emergency Oil Stocks as an Option to Respond to Oil Supply Disruptions, 2002.

Australian Department of Foreign Affairs and Trade (DFAT). "Economic Costs of Terrorism". DFAT Economic Analytical Unit, Global Issues Brief, 7 April 2003.

————. The Costs of Maritime Terrorism and Piracy and the Benefits of Working Together. Paper presented to the APEC High-level meeting on Maritime Security and Cooperation, 8–9 September 2003, Manila.

Australian APEC Study Centre. Proceedings of the Symposium of Maritime Experts to Assist in Implementation of the Secure Trade in the APEC Region (STAR) Initiative, 18–20 June 2003, Melbourne. <www.apec.org.an/STAR-Symposium/Home.asp>.

Barnaby, Frank. *How to Build a Nuclear Bomb and Other Weapons of Mass Destruction*. London: Granta Books.

Bateman, Sam. Maritime Security: A New Environment Following September 11. Paper presented to the Symposium of Maritime Experts to Assist in Implementation of the Apec STAR Initiative, Melbourne, 18–20 June 2003.

————. Sea Lane Security. Paper presented to the APEC High-level Meeting on Maritime Security and Cooperation, Manila, 8–9 September, 2003.

Beckman, Robert C. Enhancing Maritime Security in the Straits of Malacca and Singapore. Paper presented to the conference on Securing the Oceans, Institute for Ocean Policy, Ship & Ocean Foundation, Tokyo, 17–18 October, 2003.

Bunn, Matthew. Preventing Nuclear Terrorism: A Progress Update. The Nuclear Threat Initiative and the Project on Managing the Atom in the Belfer Center for Science and International Affairs, John F. Kennedy School of Government, Harvard University, 22 October 2003.

Burnett, John S. *Dangerous Waters: Modern Piracy and Terror on the High Seas*. New York: Plume, 2002.

Carafano, J.J. and Jack Spencer. Dealing with Dirty Bombs; Plain Facts, Practical Solutions. Heritage Foundation Background Paper no. 1723, 27 January 2004.

Chalk, Peter. Liberation Tigers of Tamil Eelam's (LTTE) International Organization and Operations — A Preliminary Analysis. Canadian Security Intelligence Service. *Commentary* no. 77, 17 March 2000.

Chan, Danny. Modern Maritime Threats and Strategies. Paper presented at the Institute for Defence and Strategic Studies (IDSS), Singapore, 16 October 2003.

Chia Lin Sien, Mark Goh and Jose Tongzon. *Southeast Asian Regional Port Development: A Comparative Analysis*. Singapore: Institute of Southeast Asian Studies, 2003.

Churchill, Robin R. with Christopher Hedley. The Meaning of the "Genuine Link" Requirement in Relation to the Nationality of Ships. Cardiff Law School, University of Wales, October 2000.

Centre for International Security and Cooperation (CISAC). Container Security Report. Stanford Study Group, Stanford University, January 2003.

Council for Security Cooperation in the Asia Pacific (CSCAP). The Practice of the Law of the Sea in the Asia Pacific. Memorandum no. 6, Council for Security Cooperation in the Asia Pacific, December 2002.

Davidson, Scott. The Legal Framework for Enhancing Maritime Security. Paper presented to the joint meeting of the Council for Security Cooperation in Asia Pacific (CSCAP) and the Pacific Economic Cooperation Council, Manila, 6–7 September 2003.

Dillon, Dana R. The War on Terrorism in Southeast Asia: Developing Law Enforcement. Heritage Foundation Background Paper no. 1720, 22 January 2004.

Economist. Special Report on Container Trade. "When Trade and Security Clash", 4 April 2002.

―――. Special Report on Proliferation. "A World Wide Web of Nuclear Danger", 28 February 2004.

European Commission. Proposal for a Directive of the European Parliament and of the Council on Enhancing Port Security, 2 May 2003.

Feinstein, Lee and Anne-Marie Slaughter. "A Duty to Prevent: Disarming Rogues". *Foreign Affairs*, January/February 2004.

Ferguson, Charles D., Tochseen Kazi and Judith Perera, "Commercial Radioactive Sources: Surveying the Security Risks". Centre for Nonproliferation Studies, Monterey Institute for International Studies. Occasional Paper no. 11, <www.cns.miis.edu/pubs/opapers/op11>.

Fox, John G. Sea Change: Strategic Consequences of the Transformation of World Shipping. US National Defence University, National War College, <www.ndu.edu/nwc/>.

Group of Eight. Global Partnership Update, Interparliamentary Conference Edition, November 2003, <www.sgpprojects.org>.

Gunaratna, Rohan. *Inside Al Qaeda: Global Network of Terror*. London: C. Hurst & Co, 2002.

Institute for Ocean Policy and the East-West Center. The Regime of the Exclusive Economic Zone: Issues and Responses. Summary report of a meeting of senior officials and analysts, Tokyo, 19–20 February 2003.

International Atomic Energy Agency (IAEA). Nuclear Security — Measures to Protect Against Nuclear Terrorism. Report by the IAEA director general to the agency's general conference, 20 August 2003.

————. "Towards a Safer World", by IAEA Director General Mohamed ElBaradei, *Economist*, 16 October 2003.

————. "Saving Ourselves from Self-Destruction", by Mohamed ElBaradei, *New York Times*, 12 February 2004.

————. Promoting Nuclear Security: What the IAEA is Doing, <www.iaea.org>.

International Crisis Group. Jemaah Islamiyah in South East Asia: Damaged but still Dangerous. Report no. 63, 26 August 2003.

International Maritime Organisation (IMO). Maritime Security. Paper on "ownership" and "control" of ships submitted by the United States of America to the IMO Legal Committee, 26 March 2002.

International Transport Workers' Federation (ITF). Flags of Convenience Campaign Update. <www.itf.org.uk>, September 2003.

————. Flags of Convenience Campaign Report 2001/02. <www.itf.org.uk>, July 2002.

Japanese Shipowners' Association. Report on the Current State of Japanese Shipping, March 2003.

Langewiesche, William. "Anarchy at Sea". *Atlantic Monthly*, September 2003.

Lim, Irvin. "Fireball on the Water: Naval Force Protection-Projection, Coast Guarding, Customs Border Security and Multilateral Cooperation in Rolling Back the Global Waves of Terror from the Sea". IDSS Working Paper no. 53. Singapore: Institute for Defence and Strategic Studies. 2003.

Mak, J.N. Port and Trade Security after 9/11: The Challenges Ahead. Paper presented at the 13th Meeting of the CSCAP Maritime Cooperation Working Group, Manila, 6–7 September 2003.

Mitropoulos, E.E. The Work of IMO on Maritime Security: Outcome of the 2002 SOLAS Conference. Paper presented at the APEC High-Level Meeting on Maritime Security Cooperation, 8–9 September 2003, Manila.

Nikitin, Mary Beth. Global Partnership Basics. Center for Strategic and International Studies, Washington, August 2003.

Nunn, Sam. Kazakhstan: Reducing Nuclear Dangers, Increasing Global Security. 16 December 2003.

Organisation for Economic Co-operation and Development (OECD). "Report on Ownership and Control of Ships", Paris: OECD, March 2003.

————. "Report on Security in Maritime Transport: Risk Factors and Economic Impact". Paris: OECD, July 2003.

Ong, C. Gerard. Ships can be Dangerous Too: Coupling Piracy and Terrorism in Southeast Asia's Maritime Security Framework. Paper prepared for the People and the Sea II Conference, Centre for Maritime Research and the International Institute for Asian Studies Amsterdam, 4–6 September 2003.

Potter, William C., Charles D. Ferguson and Leonard S. Spector, "The Four Faces of Nuclear Terror and the Need for a Prioritized Response". *Foreign Affairs* 83, no. 3 (May/June 2004): 1–3.

Rabasa, Angel M. *Political Islam in Southeast Asia: Moderates, Radicals and Terrorists*. Adelphi Paper 358. London: International Institute for Strategic Studies, May 2003.

Shipping Industry Guidelines on Flag State Performance. Round Table of International Shipping Industry Organisations, November 2003.

Stern, Jessica. "The Protean Enemy: What's Next from Al Qaeda". *Foreign Affairs*, July/August 2003.

Tongue, Andrew. Meeting Maritime Obligations Under STAR and IMO, presentation to Symposium of Maritime Experts to Assist in the Implementation of the APEC STAR Initiative, Melbourne, 18–20 June 2003.

United Nations Conference on Trade and Development (UNCTAD). "Review of Maritime Transport". Geneva: UNCTAD, 7 November 2003.

US Coast Guard. Maritime Strategy for Homeland Security. <www.uscg.mil>, December 2002.

US Department of Energy. World Oil Transit Chokepoints. Country Analysis Brief. November 2002.

Vander Voort, Martin, Kevin A. O'Brien, Adnan Rahman and Lorenzo Valeri. Seacurity: Improving the Security of the Global Sea-Container Shipping System. Leiden, Berlin, Cambridge: RAND Europe, 8 September 2003.

World Shipping Council. About the Council, Partners in America's Trade. <www.worldshipping.org/abo.html.>.

————. Comments on Operation Safe Commerce submitted to the Transportation Security Administration of the US Department of Transportation, 5 December 2002.

Wrightson, Margaret. Maritime Security: Progress Made in Implementing Maritime Transportation Security Act, but Concerns Remain. Statement of Director, Homeland Security and Justice Issues, before the US Senate Committee on Commerce, Science and Transportation, 9 September 2003.

About the Author

Michael Richardson, former Asia Editor of the *International Herald Tribune*, is a Visiting Senior Research Fellow at the Institute of Southeast Asian Studies, Singapore. His current research focuses on maritime, energy and sealane security. The views expressed, and the recommendations made, in this book are those of the author. He welcomes comments.

Telephone: 65–64791356
E-mail: mriht@pacific.net.sg

Printed in the United States
81956LV00004B/142